"A refreshingly hopeful book, at once pastoral and personal. Tony Scarcello does more than simply show where we've gone wrong. He reminds us that the way of Jesus is still good and beautiful news for every single one of our neighbors—and for us."

Gregory Coles, author of *Single, Gay, Christian* and *No Longer Strangers*

"Tony Scarcello's *Love All Our Neighbors* is the book I've been waiting to be able to shout out from the rooftops about. Tony's story—compounded by rich theological conviction and brutal compassion—offers the church a way forward that cuts through the muck. Tony's is a voice in the wilderness that deserves to be heard. You would be wise to listen."

A.J. Swoboda, associate professor of Bible and theology at Bushnell University and author of *Slow Theology*

"I will never understand why those of us who experience same-sex attractions and surrender them to Jesus experience greater scrutiny than those who experience another form of sexual brokenness. Tony Scarcello graciously helps us examine some of the problems and solutions to this issue so we can worship Jesus together."

Laurie Krieg, author of *Raising Wise Kids in a Sexually Broken World*

"Navigating tension with both conviction and kindness seems like a skill that's in sadly short supply these days. But in *Love All Our Neighbors*, Tony Scarcello shows us how. This book weaves together theological richness, biblical conviction, pastoral nuance, and deep human kindness to show us how we might embody Christlike love to any and all God brings into our spheres of influence."

Jay Y. Kim, pastor and author of *Analog Christian* and *Analog Church*

"This book offers far more than the perspective of an intelligent thinker with strong ideals—it comes from someone shaped by deeply lived experiences. Tony Scarcello provides a thoughtful, compassionate guide that will help many Christians learn to love and understand their LGBTQ neighbors more fully. The church needs Scarcello's voice in this conversation."

Andrew Damazio, lead pastor of The Rose Church

"There is little question that Christianity in the United States has largely harmed LGBTQ+ people. But love offers a better way than demonization, alienation, or non-engagement. Tony Scarcello's honesty, vulnerability, experience, and insights can help many Christians—especially those who hold to traditional heterosexual views of sexual relationships and marriage. *Love All Our Neighbors* invites us all to look at ourselves while we reach out to others."

Dennis R. Edwards, seminary dean, vice president for church relations at North Park Theological Seminary, and author of *Humility Illuminated*

"*Love All Our Neighbors* has a very rare, powerful combo when talking about this critically sensitive and über-important topic. First, Tony Scarcello shares his firsthand experience, showing this isn't theoretical talk but from one who understands what he is writing about. Second, we see a solid grounding in the historical doctrines of the Christian faith and ethics without compromise to the culture. It is crystal clear the answer is not rethinking Scripture to compromise truth as many have done. Third, it is a book of heart, compassion, and love—not angry, pointing fingers, creating a battle—with the goal of redemption, reconciliation, restoration, and the gospel changing lives."

Dan Kimball, vice president of Western Seminary and author of *How (Not) to Read the Bible*

"Tony Scarcello has walked a hard, narrow path with grace, love, and truth. In *Love All Our Neighbors* he leads the way to help others do the same. This book will challenge you. It may make you uncomfortable at times. It will definitely make you think. But mostly it will equip you to wrestle through hard realities with the kind of grace, truth, and love Tony embodies in his life and ministry."

Karen Swallow Prior, author of *You Have a Calling: Finding your Vocation in Truth, Goodness, and Beauty*

"I'm so grateful this book exists. Tony Scarcello has impacted my life deeply as a friend, and it's a gift to see his hard-earned wisdom now shared with the world. *Love All Our Neighbors* avoids pat answers and tired clichés, modeling the life-changing combination of grace and truth—orthodoxy expressed with compassion. It is a faithful and needed guide for the church as we learn to love our LGBTQ+ neighbors well."

Joshua Ryan Butler, teaching pastor with the Willamette family of churches and author of *God Is on Your Side* and *The Party Crasher*

HOW CHURCHES THAT HOLD A TRADITIONAL SEXUAL ETHIC CAN CARE FOR LGBTQ PEOPLE

LOVE ALL OUR NEIGHBORS

TONY SCARCELLO

Foreword by Preston Sprinkle

An imprint of InterVarsity Press
Downers Grove, Illinois

InterVarsity Press
P.O. Box 1400 | Downers Grove, IL 60515-1426
ivpress.com | email@ivpress.com

InterVarsity Press® is the publishing division of InterVarsity Christian Fellowship/USA®. For more information, visit intervarsity.org.

Cover design: Faceout Studio, Addie Lutzo
Interior design: Daniel van Loon
Cover images: © TheMountBirdStudio / iStock via Getty Images Plus; © Valentin Agapov via Shutterstock

ISBN 978-1-5140-1087-7 (print) | ISBN 978-1-5140-1088-4 (digital)

Printed in the United States of America ♾

Library of Congress Cataloging-in-Publication Data
Names: Scarcello, Anthony Wayne, 1991- author
Title: Love all our neighbors : how churches that hold a traditional sexual ethic can care for LGBTQ people / Tony Scarcello.
Description: Downers Grove, IL : IVP, [2026] | Includes biographical information. | Includes bibliographical references.
Identifiers: LCCN 2025054405 (print) | LCCN 2025054406 (ebook) | ISBN 9781514010877 paperback | ISBN 9781514010884 ebook
Subjects: LCSH: Homosexuality–Religious aspects–Christianity | Love–Religious aspects–Christianity | Church work with gay people
Classification: LCC BR115.H6 S33 2026 (print) | LCC BR115.H6 (ebook)
LC record available at https://lccn.loc.gov/2025054405
LC ebook record available at https://lccn.loc.gov/2025054406

33 32 31 30 29 28 27 26 | 13 12 11 10 9 8 7 6 5 4 3 2 1

Dedicated to my mother in-law,

Carole "Ma" Blancher.

Thank you for ten years of working hard to love

and understand me. You modeled so much

of what this book aims for.

I can't wait to see you again with your fancy new legs.

CONTENTS

Foreword

PRESTON SPRINKLE

I'll never forget meeting Tony for the first time at a pub in his hometown where I happened to be speaking. His magnetic personality and intentional posture instantly convinced me: We were going to be lifelong friends. I was most impressed by his relentless passion for theological orthodoxy and his unswerving desire to reach marginalized people. I've found this to be a rare combo. I've met many Christians over the years who are thrilled to talk about one or the other, but Tony was electrified by both. He seamlessly shared his excitement about the latest theological book he was wading through and his enthusiasm to reach the lonely kid in the youth group whom no one wants to befriend. Meeting Tony gave me a glimpse into the heart of Jesus.

And then he told me his story. It left me on the brink of tears. He tells it in this book, so I won't give it away. Let's just say, Tony has had every reason to denounce Jesus and walk away from the church. Instead he has become more passionate than ever to celebrate the supremacy of Jesus and embody Jesus' heart in leaving the ninety-nine to go after the one. Tony is, therefore, the perfect person to lead us in conversations about faith, sexuality, and gender.

Tony is one of those rare individuals who has lived on both sides of the pulpit—as a congregant overwhelmed by fear and shame wrestling with his own sexuality and as a pastor ministering the love of Jesus to others who are wondering if the traditional sexual ethic is both true and livable. In *Love All Our Neighbors*, Tony brings his own lived experience to the table to help us navigate the beautiful tension of celebrating God's good design for marriage and sexuality while reaching those on the margins who are questioning whether God has a place for them in his church. Tony shatters the misperception that a traditional sexual ethic is an insurmountable barrier that stands between LGBTQ people and Jesus. Grace and truth are not at odds. Like two wings on an airplane, both are vital for flight and faithfulness.

But how do we do this? This is where the pastoral rubber meets the road. Many Christians affirm grace and truth. We believe the Bible. We believe in love. But practically speaking, how do we do this with LGBTQ people? Is it possible to believe, promote, and celebrate a traditional sexual ethic and truly love, value, and include LGBTQ people in the flourishing life of the church? Can Christian parents truly love their LGBTQ kid without sacrificing their beliefs? Can we actually preach the truth and also extend love toward LGBTQ people?

To summarize Tony's wonderful book—yes. Yes we can. It's not only possible but necessary: to believe what Jesus said about marriage and sexuality and to embody Jesus' radical welcome to those around us, especially those who have been dehumanized by the church.

In *Love All Our Neighbors*, you'll receive more than theoretical statements about grace and truth. As you journey with Tony in this book, you'll feel as Tony felt when he was shamed and shunned by well-meaning Christians. You will understand how the church has placed unnecessary barriers between LGBTQ people and the gospel. You will learn how to practically love LGBTQ people while holding true to what the Bible says about sexuality. In *Love All Our Neighbors*, you will experience the heart of Jesus.

INTRODUCTION

We who formerly hated and murdered one another and did not even share our heart with those of a different tribe because of their customs, now, after Christ's appearance, live together and share the same table. Now we pray for our enemies and try to win those who hate us unjustly so that they too may live in accordance with Christ's wonderful teachings, that they too may enter into the expectation, that they too may receive the same good things that we will receive from God, the Ruler of the universe.

Justin the Martyr

You are a gift to the church. Without you the church loses some of its beauty, power, and function. The truth is, when you became a Christian and a part of the church, you didn't sign on for a decaying institution in Western culture. Rather you became part of a highly complex and highly alive organism called the body of Christ. And the church is better because you are a part of it.

Yes, you are flawed, occasionally self-centered, sometimes unwise, and often miss the mark, but the church is more what God dreamed of it to be with you in it. You have gifts, contributions, critiques, and passions the church needs. You came to Christ in raggedy clothes with a prodigal spirit, and Christ redeemed you and released you into the mission of heaven.

The same can be true for our LGBTQ+ neighbors.

However, tragically, many churches have proven not to be a safe or viable option for them. When I realized my own same-sex attraction, I felt like more of a burden to the church than a gift. Many LGBTQ+ people feel similarly. There is a chasm where there ought to be reconciliation.

One of my favorite portions of the apostle Paul's writings in the New Testament reads:

> So from now on we regard no one from a worldly point of view. Though we once regarded Christ in this way, we do so no longer. Therefore, if anyone is in Christ, the new creation has come: The old has gone, the new is here! All this is from God, who reconciled us to himself through Christ and gave us the ministry of reconciliation: that God was reconciling the world to himself in Christ, not counting people's sins against them. And he has committed to us the message of reconciliation. We are therefore Christ's ambassadors, as though God were making his appeal through us. (2 Corinthians 5:16-20)

What a staggering call.

Paul's admonition that we are to "regard no one from a worldly point of view" implies that we are to regard everyone from a heavenly point of view. When we interact with our LGBTQ+ neighbors we are not interacting with an ideology, political movement, social media post, movie caricature, or bill being debated in Congress. We are interacting with people, made in the image of God, whom our Savior bled and died to redeem. We are interacting with people God loved literally to the point of his own death. When we regard people from a worldly point of view, that is a surefire sign our muddy biases and ideologies have eclipsed the redeeming radiance of the cross.

These verses also state that Christ has given us the "ministry of reconciliation." This task of reconciling God with his children, inaugurated by Jesus, is now given to believers. Christ the King wants to be reconciled to a world severed from him, and he has appointed us as ambassadors for the task. God's preferential method for reconciling humanity back to him is you, and me, and the rest of the body of Christ. This means that for followers of Jesus, one of our primary postures toward the world is that of reconciler.

When I was younger and first joining the ministry, I believed God wanted soldiers in his army to defend him against post-modern secularists. I had a zealous fire to defend God and shoot down untruth wherever I came across it. After fifteen years of ministry and twenty years of reading and rereading Scripture, I now know God is not looking for soldiers to defend him. He does not need defending; he defends us. He is looking for beloved partnership in the ministry of reconciliation.

The church is more than a gathering; it is meant to be a people whose lives have been caught up in the way of Jesus. We are a colony of heaven planted in the soil of earth, leaning toward the dawn of new creation—with the risen Christ the first fruits of its harvest. We stand as his ambassadors, carrying resurrection in our bones. Reconciled by grace, we are sent as reconcilers. And through this fragile, radiant community, the God of the universe whispers and thunders his appeal: Behold my beauty, taste my goodness, know my love. And yet sometimes we actively harm vulnerable people while trying to be a reconciler. LGBTQ+ people have been consistent casualties of this unintended harm. And it can feel as if there is no way to reconcile without more hurt. Or if there is a way, it feels to many that there is no turning the tide on the harm already done.

In a world where culture wars have created casualties on both sides of the political aisle, where political tribalism threatens to tear the church apart, where secular sexual ethics are not just accepted but considered the only moral option, where postmodern gender theory is widely embraced, where many wonder if the church has anything meaningful to offer the world anymore, where disagreement is grounds for terminating relationships, where some states seek to restrict parental rights if they refuse to grant children gender reassignment care and other states seek to restrict their rights if they do . . . in this world, is it possible for orthodox Christian churches to become places where LGBTQ+ people don't just show up but thrive?

Some may dismiss this as a naive dream. But I am convinced it is not only possible, it is necessary. It is a holy imperative. And I see a new imagination rising: followers of Jesus stirred with longing to live out the holy imperative. Captivated by his love, his embrace, his radical welcome, they ache to see the church mirror Christ's love—wide enough, deep enough, fierce enough—for everyone.

WHAT THIS BOOK IS NOT

In an age of virtue signaling and bitter polarization, clarity is essential. Whenever I speak about the church and our LGBTQ+ neighbors, there is inevitably at least one person who is quick to project political motives onto me. Their allegiance to their partisan tribes deafens them to what I am saying, and they assign assumptions that often drown out my words.

So I need to be clear. This book is not a partisan manifesto. It does not peddle a liberal vision of culture-warring, nor does it toe the conservative party line.

I have no interest in baptizing diversity-and-inclusion slogans, just as I have no interest in rallying behind reactionary rhetoric. If a phrase in these pages sounds like a dog whistle to one camp or the other, hear me clearly: It is not. The aims of this book stretch beyond the narrow trenches of our political battles. They cannot be contained by the myopic categories of left or right.

WHAT THIS BOOK IS

My concern is not culture war, but Christ. Not slogans, but the gospel. Not ideology, but the way of Jesus—full of grace and full of truth. Christ started and ended his incarnated ministry with magnificent proclamations such as "The kingdom of God has come near. Repent and believe the good news" and "You will receive power when the Holy Spirit comes on you; and you will be my witnesses" (Mark 1:15; Acts 1:8). When it comes to heeding these words for our LGBTQ+ neighbors, the church has often fallen tragically short. We need churches to remove the significant and harmful barriers that are keeping LGBTQ+ people at bay.

These barriers range from subtle to overt, and they have been baked into the fabric of many faith communities thanks to culture wars, tribalism, troubling ideas about God, and our own fear of "the other." Time and again I have seen church leaders change their language in the pulpit when discussing LGBTQ+ people but fail to address the barriers in the community that result in deep pain for LGBTQ+ people. The pastor may actively discourage homophobic slurs and avoid "Adam-and-Eve-not-Adam-and-Steve" hackneyed clichés, but many in the congregation have been discipled for decades by other voices to treat LGBTQ+ people with fear and suspicion, even those committed to the Bible's vision for sex, marriage, and gender.

In fact, this fear and suspicion of our LGBTQ+ neighbors has kept many church people from acknowledging that there are LGBTQ+ people in theological alignment with the historic perspective on these things. There are gay or same-sex-attracted Christians who actively resist their sexual desires out of obedience to Jesus. There are Christians who experience incongruence between their inner sense of self and their physical bodies (gender dysphoria) but who press forward in faithful discipleship.

There are many, many unheard and unseen LGBTQ+ Christians.

It is the core conviction of this book that many followers of Jesus want to see LGBTQ+ people embraced by the radical love of God. The intention of God revealed in Scripture is that this embrace would happen in our churches. It can be this way. We just need a little help getting there.

I have spent the last several years traveling everywhere from California to Pennsylvania to Ontario in Canada helping churches, leaders, believers, and parents figure out how to love the LGBTQ+

people in their lives even as they hold to a traditional sexual ethic. This book pulls from those experiences and is my humble attempt to help equip followers of Jesus on this journey.

What follows is my best attempt to do four things:

- Examine the tension churches often feel between loving LGBTQ+ people and remaining committed to the historical Christian sexual ethic.
- See how churches have failed to love, minster to, and effectively reach their LGBTQ+ neighbors and instead built barriers that keep LGBTQ+ people at a distance.
- Uncover the reason for these barriers, as well as the historical moments, trends, and ideas that got us here.
- Explore practical guidance and theological convictions that can help us move forward. We will look at examples of prominent leaders who have loved and received LGBTQ+ people without discarding the historic, traditional stance on sex, gender, and marriage, and we will cast a vision for a church witness that is full of grace and truth.

This book is not intended to be a comprehensive theological exploration of the ethics or science of same-sex unions and gender transitions, although we will examine these matters along the way. Nor is it strictly a memoir chronicling my own story as a same-sex-attracted Christian. This work intends to explore how disciples of Jesus can do in the church for LGBTQ+ people what has been done in the church for other broken people in need of Jesus: Remove the barriers between Jesus and the people who need him, and create spaces where everyone is invited to thrive in the body of Christ.

THE URGENCY OF THE MOMENT

Entering into this conversation can be daunting for some, but we ignore it at great cost. This topic is not going away. The existence of people who experience attraction to the same sex or gender dysphoria won't be prayed away, thrown away, or ignored forever. More people every year are identifying somewhere within the LGBTQ+ paradigm. Recently, a poll revealed that upward of 30 percent of Gen Z identifies somewhere within the LGBTQ+ experience.[1] Sooner or later, this topic will become personal for you. At some point, you or someone you love is going to understand what it is like. If you're reading this, you or someone you love likely already does.

The church is left with a few options on how to respond. We can put our heads in the sand and never address it, but in so doing we will leave it to an unredeemed world to lead the conversation instead. We can take up arms and try to fight it, but, as we will see in a later chapter, this will do more harm than good and compromise our witness. Or we can be like Jesus. While the growing number of people identifying as LGBTQ+ might sound alarming to many inside the church, there is also much to hope for. These people have the same aching hunger for Christ we all do.

The church must recover a missional imagination for our LGBTQ+ neighbors—helping them, like all of us, find and follow Jesus. Not only those outside our walls but also the many already within who love Jesus. They are not outsiders but members of Christ's body, grafted in by the same redeeming cross and welcomed into the same family. Yes, the shape of self-denial, cross-bearing, and repentance will look different for LGBTQ+ believers than for straight believers. But difference is the beauty of the body.

We are all invited to follow Jesus with a limp. And when the whole church limps together toward the kingdom, the world begins to shimmer with the holy fire of God's love.

The conversation about LGBTQ+ people and the church is messy, tangled with pain and misunderstanding. It is full of theological complexity and a sordid history where the church has frequently failed to reflect Jesus. Yet it is precisely into this mess that Christ calls his people to bear witness—patiently, humbly, and with the relentless hope of resurrection

It is not too late for LGBTQ+ people outside the church to find and follow Jesus, and it is not too late for the church to help them. If we don't get serious about cultivating spaces where our LGBTQ+ neighbors can bring their whole stories to the table and be called to the cross-carrying, self-denying, life-discovering way of Jesus, we won't care for those currently in church either.

The church is the beloved community of God. It is the physical representation of Christ on the earth. It is a community of love, belonging, holiness, affection, repentance, hope, forgiveness, and grace. Church has not always felt like this for many LGBTQ+ Christians. It's time for the church to be church for everybody.

1

THE FELT TENSION

Truth does not change according to our ability to stomach it.

FLANNERY O'CONNOR

The idea of me writing a book like this felt impossible a decade ago. I spent the first twenty-three years of my life hiding my same-sex attraction from everyone. It was a secret embedded with crippling shame. Somehow, through God's mysterious affinity for redeeming stories, here I am. Not only writing this book but having spent much of the past five years watching God leverage my pain and shame for the healing of others.

A few months ago, I spoke on my story and the Christian sexual ethic at a conference. I shared the bitter pain that came with experiencing same-sex attraction in conservative Christian spaces and how it nearly cost me my life. But I also shared about the beauty and transcendence of God's design for male and female in marriage, known as the traditional sexual ethic. I ended my talk with a plea: Embody a grace that heals the wounds of shame, and advocate for the truth that God has defined marriage and gender with exquisite intention. We redefine marriage and gender at our own peril, no matter how honest our motives may be.

After the session ended, people lingered to talk, ask questions, share encouragement. Then, as things quieted down, a man (another pastor) approached me. He waited until the crowd had thinned, then walked up slowly with a heaviness in his eyes.

"Thanks for your message," he said, and paused. "It was faithful . . . and I needed to hear it. But can I be honest with you?"

"Of course," I said.

He took a beat, then said, "I have LGBTQ+ people I care about in my congregation. I've sat in their living rooms. I've watched them cry. I've had to repent of my own homophobia. And I don't know how to love them well while maintaining a traditional ethic. I feel like the traditional ethic is a betrayal to them."

He looked away for a second, then back at me, and named a tension many of us feel.

"It feels like no matter what I say, or don't say, I'm failing someone. So lately, I've just gone quiet. And that silence . . . it's starting to feel like cowardice. But I still don't know what to do. The traditional ethic feels so unloving sometimes."

THE PROGRESSIVE POSITION IS NOT A MAGIC ELIXIR

There is a common tension many of us feel in this conversation. It seems to some that in order to be truly loving, we must embrace a progressive vision of sexuality and gender and discard the traditional one. Others discard being loving in order to embrace the traditional vision. To frame the traditional ethic against authentic love is a false dichotomy. But that hasn't stopped it from gaining steam in recent years.

A while ago I was at the Washburn Café, the best coffee shop in Springfield, Oregon, for those in the know. I sat across from an old friend who identified as progressive. I, along with a stellar team, had recently planted Open Table Church. This friend wanted to know our church's stance on LGBTQ+ issues.

I told him our church believed that Jesus' table was big enough for all of our stories, that we worked hard to love anyone who came through our door, and that we prayed every Sunday that we would receive whoever joined us just as Jesus had received us. I told him that experiencing same-sex attraction myself had made me ultra-aware of how churches can be uniquely precarious places for LGBTQ+ people and that we were actively working to be a place where LGBTQ+ people could thrive. I also told him our church held to the historic, traditional view of sex and marriage.

"So, you're a non-affirming church?" he asked.

I hate that term, *non-affirming*. I don't believe my views on what someone does with their genitals determines whether or not I affirm their entire personhood. The term is indicative of our cultural moment, though. We are so defined by our sexual interests that to not affirm what someone does with their sexuality is to not affirm their personhood. The truth that we are more than who we want to sleep with gets lost in the discourse. Intentionally or not, the discourse reduces our humanity to sexual desire. And it seems that many of us are all too willing to let our humanity be reduced to what we desire.

Now, to be clear, I do not advocate a Buddhist-style renunciation of desire. When properly ordered and understood, desire is key to human flourishing. In his book *The Gift of Thorns*, A. J. Swoboda makes a strong case that human beings have the capacity for desire not because of original sin but because their Creator experiences desire. Swoboda writes:

> Given how central repentance, holiness, and self-denial are to Christian spirituality, one could uncritically presume that Christianity and desire are inherently hostile. But does this hold up? To Scripture? Or to the way of Jesus? . . . These ideas are as half-baked today as they ever were. Not only this, but they're detached from reality and dangerous to the human soul. We were made to desire. To be desire*less* is inhumane.[1]

Desire is not in and of itself bad. Desire in its purest form is a gift. However, until our deepest desire is for God himself, we must never forget that we are much more than what we desire.

But I knew my friend was not looking for that soapbox. So I answered his question honestly.

"We affirm what Scripture has taught, that sex is intended for a biological man and a biological woman in the covenantal union of marriage."

He looked at me like I'd just told him we should go kick some kittens. Then he said, "The only church safe for LGBTQ+ people is an affirming church. Non-affirming churches are deadly to queer people. You can do everything you want to welcome queer people, but unless you're affirming, nothing else you do will matter."

I thought this was an audacious claim for a heterosexual agnostic to make to a same-sex attracted pastor. I let my heterosexual progressive friend vent his misgivings about how toxic my church would be to his gay friends. I genuinely listened. And honestly? I understood where he was coming from. His concern is shared by many well-meaning progressive voices both inside and outside the church.

A common belief among progressives is that we have to sever ourselves from the historic theological perspective on gender and sexuality to genuinely love and serve LGBTQ+ people. I myself spent many years wrestling with this tension. However, I have become convinced that it's misleading to call the historic theological perspective inherently harmful.

The largest scientific survey ever conducted of LGBTQ+ people and their religious backgrounds debunked the assertion that the progressive perspective is the only safe one. In this survey, it was discovered that 81 percent of LGBTQ+ people grew up in a faith community, and 51 percent left after turning eighteen. And, shockingly, of the 51 percent who left, only 21 percent did so over theological disagreements.[2] They were far more likely to leave because of negative experiences such as homophobia or because they were kicked out, felt unsafe, or weren't being allowed to contribute. Even the 21 percent who left over theological misgivings didn't always leave because they disagreed with the church's theology of sex and marriage.[3]

One gay man said, "I left the church because I couldn't find one person who would listen to my story, really listen." A gay couple said, "We never expected this church to conduct our marriage ceremony. We just wanted them to love our kids like any other kid."[4]

The narrative is often framed as "Christians who hold a traditional sexual ethic harm gay people." But is this universally true? Is it the ethic held or the way we hold it? Many times, this question isn't given its due diligence. Preston Sprinkle writes, "Sweeping generalizations like 'Christians' and 'gay people' are very unhelpful—as if every gay person is harmed by every Christian who holds to a traditional marriage ethic. What about the hundreds of thousands of gay people who believe in a historically Christian view on marriage and sexual ethics? They don't say they are harmed by the theology they believe in, even if they say they've been hurt by fellow Christians with the same view."[5]

This belief, that the historic position on sex and marriage is inherently harmful, is not rooted in verifiable data. It is the product of a culture that believes humanity to be far more fragile than it is. In their searing work *The Coddling of the American Mind*, moral psychologist Jonathan Haidt and lawyer-activist Greg Lukianoff rebuke our culture's tendency to cocoon young people and guard them from challenge. Human beings are not just not fragile, they point out—they are antifragile. Challenges don't break us; they empower us. The opposite is also true: "When we protect people from risk and discomfort, we deprive them of the necessary adversities to help them grow."[6]

My point here is not that we should subject LGBTQ+ people to unnecessary risk and pain. Rather, it's that being in a room with someone who disagrees with us, even about significant matters, isn't going to hurt us. A traditional sexual ethic is not unsafe—but the posture we hold it with can be.

There are many barriers between the church and LGBTQ+ people, and adopting a progressive position on sex and marriage will not make them suddenly disappear. What's more, it's not the task of the church to upend two-thousand-year-old historic positions so it can appeal to those who find said positions offensive. It is, however, the task of the church to represent Jesus to the world, be ministers of reconciliation, and bear witness to the goodness, beauty, and love of Jesus.

And yet when we hear a statement like this—"Marriage, defined by Scripture, applies only to opposite-sexed biological males and females in lifelong covenantal union"—it's easy to feel discouraged by how exclusive it is. The problem is that the conversation is framed in such a way that it robs the traditional sexual ethic (and a healthy theology of the body, for that matter) of its beauty and context. This is why it feels unloving. Before we go any further, we must recover the beauty of God's created order from underneath the rubble of violent fundamentalism and ignorant progressivism.

TRADITIONAL ETHIC

This is not a comprehensive review of the traditional ethic, as there are several rich theological works exploring this topic.[7] What I'd like to do here instead is unpack what we mean by "traditional ethic" and why there is beauty to be found in it. A corrective is necessary, since the loudest voices defining the traditional ethic have come either from hardhearted, anxious, outraged fundamentalists or from wounded, reactive, revisionist progressives.

Neither group has charitably or accurately captured the beauty and context of the traditional ethic. Despite how harsh fundamentalists might make it sound, God's created order tells the most beautiful, hopeful, loving story in history. And despite what defensive progressivism might say, God does have a well-defined, thoroughly understandable ethic.

When people discuss sexual ethics, particularly concerning same-sex relationships, the conversation often centers on what the Bible prohibits. This is the wrong place to start. Before we ask whether the Bible forbids same-sex marriage or gender transition, we must ask deeper, more foundational questions: What does Scripture say marriage is? What does Scripture teach about our bodies? For followers of Jesus, boundaries are not about restriction but about revelation: God revealing his design for creation, covenant, and, ultimately, human flourishing.

In 1 Corinthians 7, Paul addresses issues of sexuality, celibacy, and marriage in the early church. It's important to note what Paul assumes: that sexual intimacy belongs within the covenant of marriage. That assumption is not arbitrary; it reflects a deeply rooted theology of creation, one that sees human sexuality as a gift to be stewarded according to God's intentions.

To understand what God's intentions are, we have to go back to the beginning, in Genesis, where the Bible tells the story of how everything began. Suspend for a moment questions about science and evolution, and you will see God is up to something magnificent here. The creation story in Genesis 1 has a poetic rhythm to it. It also has a central idea that is pivotal for understanding what God is up to: God creates the world by creating unity in diversity.

Read the creation account and you'll find God purposefully pairing things that, on paper, seem so opposite they could not possibly fit together. But that is the beauty of God's design: unity in diversity. God's power, and his prioritization of unity, means things that don't seem to go together are formed into creation, not chaos.

Imagine creation as a vast, intricate tapestry being woven by a master weaver (God). Each thread has its own color, texture, and place. Some threads are very different, almost opposites, but the weaver pulls them together side by side, weaving contrasts that create a beautiful, unified, and diverse picture.

With this central idea of unity in diversity in mind, we can see a trajectory in the story that is not merely informational; it's not accidental; it is building to something. Creation begins by taking complementary opposites and uniting them:

- ***Light and dark (Genesis 1:3-5).*** Two things that do not naturally coexist but, when united in God's transcendent design, give creation the circadian rhythms necessary to flourish.
- ***Sky and earth (Genesis 1:6-8).*** Above and below. So far apart from one another that we still don't know how far the skies are above the earth. However, when they're brought together, creation is placed within time and space, ripped from the conceptual and rooted in reality.
- ***Land and sea (Genesis 1:9-10).*** The thunderous waves of the ocean could not be more elementally different from the dry dirt of the desert, yet when married in creation they form the boundaries that make life possible. Shorelines become places of transition, provision, and beauty—harbors for life to emerge, ecosystems to thrive, and stories to begin.

- ***Sun and moon (Genesis 1:14-19).*** One blazes with fire and floods the world with light; the other is quiet, reflective, pulling tides in the night. Different though they are, they work in tandem, marking days, seasons, and the passage of time. They speak of order, balance, and a world ruled by faithful light, even in darkness.
- ***Birds and fish (Genesis 1:20-23).*** One soars through skies with feathered wings; the other darts through the depths with scales and fins. Their realms are disparate (air and water, flying and swimming), yet they fill the spaces above and below, proclaiming that even the most unalike belong in the same creation song.

Then we get to the climax of creation:

- ***Male and female (Genesis 1:27).*** This is the pairing to define all pairings. Just like the other contrasts in this chapter, man and woman are not the same. It is the differences between man and woman, not the sameness, that reveal God's priority for unity in diversity.

Ultimately, God values unity in diversity because that is the only way for us to be in relationship with him. Unity in diversity is how our space comes into contact with his space. God is very different from us. He is infinitely wise; we are only occasionally wise. He is always just, good, and true. We have a tendency toward oppression, corruption, and deceit. He is all-powerful, ruling even over nature. We are in control of little, even if we fool ourselves into believing otherwise.

God loving us into existence, we who are so very different from him, exposes his high priority for unity within difference.

We tend to love those who are most like us, make space for people with similar interests, and invite like-minded people to our tables. Our relational networks are more segregated than we often want to admit, The United States, being torn apart by political polarization, bears witness to this. But this is not so with God. He built values of unity in diversity into the very fabric of creation. The union of man and woman is his ongoing testimony of this truth.

GOD'S TAPESTRY

The dark thread next to the light thread isn't a mistake; it makes the light shine brighter.

The blue thread of the sky beside the brown thread of the earth gives shape and dimension.

The thread of the sun and the thread of the moon, the threads of birds and fish—all different, all necessary to complete the design.

And then the master weaver comes to the center of the tapestry: male and female.

These two threads are not the same color or texture. They stand out as distinct and different. Placed together, their difference forms the pattern's heart. Their difference makes the tapestry complete and vibrant. This is no accident. The weaver deliberately created a design where unity comes through diversity, not uniformity. The whole tapestry depends on the interplay of contrasts to reveal the fuller picture of God's glory.

In Genesis 2, this idea gets even clearer. The Bible says, "A man leaves his father and mother and is united to his wife, and they become one flesh" (v. 24). This "one flesh" union isn't just about physical intimacy; it's about two people becoming united in a deep, meaningful way that goes beyond emotion or biology. We call this unity marriage.

This union between man and woman is more than a relationship. It's a sacred sign pointing to something greater than itself. Just like the pairing of heaven and earth, marriage shows God's plan to bring unity in diversity.

When a man and a woman come together in marriage, they reflect God's heart for unity, not uniformity. Their relationship becomes a living picture of the union God wants to have with his creation. Marriage, then, isn't a human idea. It's God's idea. And in the Bible, this purposeful relationship always shows a man and a woman coming together in a way that tells the truth about who God is and what he's doing in the world.

N. T. Wright captures this beautifully when he writes, "The man and woman coming together are a symbol of something profoundly true of creation as a whole. Male and female together is itself a signpost pointing to that great complementarity of God's whole creation, of heaven and earth belonging together."[8]

In other words, the Bible does not present marriage as a cure for loneliness, a convenient social arrangement, or even simply a lifelong commitment between two people. It's not about fitting a mold, stepping into adulthood, or the desire for romance. It's not even a divine expectation. The Bible presents marriage as a symbol God embedded in creation to reflect his purposes.

UPPING THE ANTE

Paul takes this a step further in Ephesians 5, where he draws a breathtaking parallel between human marriage and the relationship between Christ and the church. Husbands are called to love their wives as Christ loved the church, sacrificially, redemptively, and with a life-giving love. Wives are called to respond to that love with trust and devotion, modeling the church's response to her Lord.

Don't miss this. Marriage is a union intended to proclaim a story, namely, the story of Christ's relentless faithfulness, harrowing pursuit, and self-sacrificial love for us. Marriage is not only a romantic act; it is a missional one. It proclaims fidelity, love, and grace to a world dying from lack of these things. The biblical paradigm for marriage, according to Paul, "refers to Christ and the church" (Ephesians 5:32 ESV).

In the biblical imagination, marriage is not an end in itself. It is a sign pointing to something greater. It is the gospel made visible in flesh and blood. By this logic, marriage has a missional function. It proclaims to the world the staggering love and unending faithfulness of God toward us. In a world where fidelity is scarce and self-sacrifice might seem foolish, marriage understood on Scripture's terms is a glimpse of new creation.

This symbolism continues all the way to the final pages of Scripture. In Revelation, the consummation of history is portrayed not simply as a victory or judgment but as a wedding: "The wedding of the Lamb has come, and his bride has made herself ready" (Revelation 19:7). The ultimate union is not between two people but between Christ and his redeemed people, a covenant fulfilled in glory. The Bible starts with a marriage in a garden and ends with a marriage in a garden-city (Revelation 21:2-3).

The man and the woman are different, because God and people are different, because heaven and earth are different. But when man and woman come together in marriage, they embody the unity in diversity used by God to compose creation. This unity is a sign to a deteriorating world that God and humanity will live in perfect harmony. It points to a promise that one day heaven and earth will come together in transcendent matrimony. It is a sermon married couples preach with their lives: Despite how different we are from God, he will go to the farthest lengths to rescue, redeem, and be unified with us.

Christopher West writes, "In creation, God's mystery of love became a visible reality through the union of the first man and the first woman. In redemption, that same mystery of divine love becomes a visible reality in the unbreakable union of Christ and the church."[9] Marriage tells a story not just about love between two people, but about the love that made the world and will one day remake it. This is why the church's theology of the body and its understanding of marriage matter so deeply. Our bodies are not just biological; they are theological. They expose a beautiful order behind all of creation.

In this we see that marriage and our bodies have both form and function. The form of marriage is a one-flesh union of biologically different people in lifelong covenantal relationship, and the form of our bodies is the two biologically different categories of people introduced in Scripture.[10] The function of marriage is to testify to the world of God's relentless faithfulness and unfailing love for us, even though we are different from him, and to proclaim that one day he will fully unite heaven and earth, our fundamentally different spaces. The function of our bodies is to testify to his embedded value for unity and diversity.

A PARABLE IN FLESH AND BLOOD

When we repurpose human bodies and marriage for our own purposes, we are not simply expanding the definition of marriage and gender; we are rewriting the story they tell. The creation of humanity as male and female is not a biological afterthought. Men and women are not interchangeable but distinct, and their differences are designed to reflect unity in diversity. The body itself speaks of divine truths, especially in its capacity for union, communion, and fruitfulness. Human bodies, and their covenantal union in marriage, are a sermon God preaches through creation.

While many same-sex couples demonstrate beautiful virtues like love, loyalty, courage, and even sacrificial commitment (some of my favorite love songs were written by Christian lesbian singer Brandi Carlile), Scripture does not define marriage based on emotional or moral quality alone. It defines it in terms of form and function: a covenantal, sexual union between male and female, who together embody the unending love of God and mirror the mystery of divine union.

Of course, this high vision of marriage has often been dishonored, even and especially by heterosexual couples. Divorce, infidelity, casual sex, and the commodification of bodies have marred the sacredness of marriage in countless ways. But failure to live out the ideal does not invalidate the ideal itself. On the contrary, it highlights our need to recover it. The church is not called to adjust its standards to accommodate cultural norms; it is called to lift its eyes to a greater story: one that redeems, restores, and redefines love itself.

In a culture obsessed with autonomy and self-fulfillment, the historic Christian vision of marriage and human bodies offers something different: a sign pointing beyond ourselves, a calling to mutual self-giving rooted in the Creator's design and revealing the Redeemer's love. Marriage is not a social contract. It is a sacred covenant, a parable in flesh and blood of a love that will never let us go. And our bodies are not human meat suits that conceal our true authentic selves; our bodies are exquisitely part of the real us.

As you can see, marriage and human bodies are not peripheral, secondary constructs in Scripture. They carry massive significance. As Laurie Krieg wrote in a recent Instagram post, when a book begins and ends with something (as the Bible does, beginning and ending with a wedding), it's telling you, "That's what this is about." The Bible is not about a sexual romance between two humans. It's about a divine romance between God and his people and the harrowing lengths to which he'll go to find those people when they are lost.

There are worthwhile reasons to safeguard the way Scripture reveals and defines gender, marriage, and sex. But there is also a legitimate tension between how the church has held these beliefs and how it has used them to justify treating our LGBTQ+ neighbors with indignity. In the next two chapters, we will look more closely at these indignities and harms. Holding to a traditional ethic while seeking to love well sometimes feels like an unclimbable mountain.

It's not, I promise.

REFLECTION QUESTIONS

1. What aspects of the traditional sexual ethic are most challenging to you?
2. What about the traditional sexual ethic is most compelling to you?
3. Why do we sometimes feel a tension between the traditional ethic and loving our LGBTQ+ neighbor?

2

HIDING TO BE LOVED

Late have I loved You, beauty so ancient and so new, late have I loved You!

And see, You were within and I was in the external world and sought You there, and in my unlovely state I plunged into those lovely created things which You made.

You were with me, and I was not with You. The lovely things kept me far from You, though if they did not have their existence in You, they had no existence at all.

Saint Augustine

I punched the side of our house over and over again, hitting so hard my knuckles started to bleed.

"There is no way for church to be safe for people like me! I'm done trying!" I internally screamed, the crisp fall air failing to cool my fiery temper.

A few months earlier I had accepted a position as a youth pastor at a new church. I had also recently recovered from a couple of years spent processing doubt and pain regarding my faith.

I grew up in politically conservative Pentecostalism. My first job out of high school was as a youth intern at the church I grew up in. Later, I became one of their youth pastors. I was living my dream. But I was hiding one mammoth of a secret.

For as long as I can remember I have been attracted to the same sex.

Not all people of the same sex, of course, and on at least one occasion, not *only* people of the same sex. I have been happily married to the girl of my dreams for over a decade now. We have a hard-won, beautiful marriage. But for the most part, when I experience physical attraction, it is toward people of the same sex as myself.

This secret came out four months into my marriage, while I was in my first youth pastor assignment. Even though I had never considered allowing my sexuality to compromise my fidelity to my wife or Jesus, it led to me being asked to step down. This was a double-edged sword. On the one hand, stepping down gave my wife and me space to process what my secret meant for our marriage without the pressure cooker of ministry. On the other hand, word got out about my secret, and some devastating comments and rumors began to spread. This church, full of wonderful, Jesus-loving people, included some folks who were ill-equipped to commune with someone with my particular struggle. Rumors began to spread, and bad ideas about the LGBTQ+ community caused a shift in how I was treated by some of the congregants.

My whole life I had feared that people would view me as a monster if my secret was ever discovered. When it all came out, through a few unfortunate incidents in the church, that fear seemed to be coming true. Eventually my wife and I came to the conclusion that we needed to take some time away from church. This led to a two-year season of soul-searching, questioning, anger, grief, deconstruction of my faith, and, ultimately, by the grace of God, a beautiful reconstruction of my faith.[1]

It wasn't long after putting my faith back together that I was invited to come on staff as the youth pastor at a different church in my hometown. This time I did not want to hide my story. I told the pastor, a man named Dave Lanning, before he hired me about my experience of same-sex attraction. Pastor Dave did not see this as a barrier that should prevent me from ministry, and even though his church was predominantly made up of conservative-leaning people, he hired me.

I also told him that at some point I wanted to be able to share my story with the church. Pastor Dave was hesitant. After all, I was happily married and aligned with the historic perspective on sex and marriage. To him there was no need to tell anyone. I, however, wanted to share for a number of reasons.

Chief among them was that growing up in church, I had never met or even heard of someone who experienced same-sex attraction while remaining committed to Jesus. I felt like a monster as a child, like I was disgusting, believing I was the only one in the history of the church to experience same-sex desires while still trying to follow Jesus. I bear literal scars on my arms from a few suicide attempts when I believed I was alone and abominable. So I wanted to normalize the idea that you can experience these things without being controlled by them. You can still walk in loving union with God.

I also wanted to share because I had experienced the liberation of living with nothing to hide. The fallout of my initial coming out was devastating, but after the smoke cleared, I had a few close friends who knew my story and loved me anyway. I have this wild idea that church ought to be a place of courageous vulnerability where we see and love one another the way Christ sees and loves us. And part of living in a community like that required being honest about one of the most pivotal pieces of my story.

Pastor Dave understood and agreed to let me share. And so, after a few months on staff, the Sunday came when I was to tell the church my story. I shared the piece of myself that had led to my deepest moments of shame and rejection. That Sunday morning when I woke up for church, I immediately regretted the decision to share.

Anxiety pulsated through my body. I was flooded with memories of comments and accusations the last time a church found out my secret. My fear that this would lead to a mass exodus from our church was palpable. I did not want to let my pastor down. My jaw grew sore from being clenched, my palms were sweaty, and my chest felt tight. I know now that these were all signs of unprocessed pain.

I didn't want people to think I was a monster. I just wanted anyone in the room who experienced these struggles, or loved someone who did, to know that God was still with them and for them.

Even though I carried a real anger for how I and my LGBTQ+ neighbors had been treated in religious spaces, I did my best to come across as kind and nonthreatening. I watched how I talked so I wouldn't "sound gay" and made sure not to make "feminine gestures." I affirmed the historic perspective that sex was intended for a biological male and a biological female in a lifelong, covenantal union called marriage. I assured them I would never compromise my fidelity to my wife. And I was as brave as I knew how to be in that moment.

For the most part, this church received my story warmly. I was encouraged, thanked, and embraced on the other side of it. Pastor Dave loved and led so well that morning. People seemed receptive . . . until we came into the office on Monday morning and found emails expressing significant concerns. A few families informed Pastor Dave they were leaving the church, some because they did not want their youth pastored by "a homosexual."

One prominent family made it clear: If their child was pastored by someone like me, his innocence would be at risk. They told Dave and me they didn't want their son exposed to the idea that homosexuality was anything other than a choice—or that God might not "cure" it. For them, this belief system was how they preserved his innocence. But my story stood in direct contradiction to the worldview they were determined to pass on.

That Monday night when I got home from the office I paused before going inside. I would have to tell my sweet wife that she was yet again going to be subjected to rejection and scrutiny because of my openness. I felt I was making my wife pay for my choices, and I again felt deep shame over an aspect of myself I'd never asked for and have never been able to shake. Anger overcame me so aggressively and unexpectedly that I punched the side of my house, and my knuckles bled.

I did not know what to do. My theological worldview resonated with the historic Christian ethic. I did not fit with progressivism, but there just didn't seem to be room for my story in more orthodox spaces. I felt helpless, like a man without a home. But leaving at this point did not feel like an option, not after Dave put himself out there for me. And especially not after the Spirit gently reminded me to be patient with others as God has been patient with me. It felt costly to stay but possibly more costly to leave.

Obviously, my temper tantrum and hurt feelings were blinding me to the rest of the church, who loved and embraced me. Many of them were uncomfortable with what I'd said that Sunday morning, but they chose to stay, to know me better, or at the very least to trust Pastor Dave. Pastor Dave himself, one of the most decent men I have ever known, gave me a platform to share my story. When he died several years later, his established confidence in me enabled the church to trust me to fill the pulpit as our denomination searched for a new lead pastor. His belief in me, same-sex-attracted and all, changed and redeemed the trajectory of my life.

GRAVEYARDS INSTEAD OF HOSPITALS

As I have discovered, decades of bad beliefs and practices have led to deeply ingrained barriers for LGBTQ+ people in the church. These barriers often lead to devastating consequences. I have been told by well-meaning Christians that I risk becoming a pedophile because of my sexual orientation. I've been told that I don't want all God has for me if I don't seek ex-gay/conversion therapy. I've been denied community and opportunities and accused of fishing for extramarital affairs because I shared my story publicly.

I would like to tell you these moments and comments trickled off my back like water from a duck's back, but the truth is, all of them poke at a fear I've had since I was twelve years old. It is a fear every Christian who struggles with their gender and sexual identity understands: that I am less welcome at the Lord's table than other sinners and saints because I struggle with my sexual identity.

My story is not an isolated incident. I've know many others with similar painful experiences. A few years before I mustered the courage to tell my story, when I was brand new to ministry, I supervised a team of volunteers for our thriving youth ministry. One of the volunteers was a dear friend I'll call Dan. Dan was a few years older than me, and shortly after he joined our volunteer team we went to Wendy's on a winter night. Over chili and baked potatoes, he shared with me that he struggled with same-sex attraction.

Dan had tears in his eyes as he stared at his cooling chili. This was the first Christian I had met who shared my struggle, and he was fighting like hell to follow Jesus in spite of it. I thought about saying, "Me too!" But I refrained. I wasn't ready. I don't remember what I said in response, but I know I tried to make him feel how I would have wanted to feel in his shoes. I asked him permission to tell our lead pastor, and he agreed.

The pastor then shared this information with the elders. A few of them feared Dan's attractions made him more dangerous to minors than our other adult volunteers. They agreed that Dan could continue to come to youth group to run the sound board for worship, but under no circumstances was he permitted to have any type of relationship with the youth or spiritual leadership within our ministry at all.

Dan had already been serving and investing in the youth, and this decision gutted him. It was the latest in a long line of mistreatments Dan had endured from church leaders in previous communities. Still, he tried for many years to work within the boundaries set for him. Made to feel like a pedophile, he nonetheless attended, served, and gave.

Even though what I had shared about Dan was meant to be kept confidential, people in the church gradually stopped talking to him. Friends stopped inviting him over, he was asked to step down from his role with Sunday morning worship, and he was spoken about behind closed doors with suspicion and apprehension.

I want to be clear: Aside from admitting to struggling with pornography, Dan had done nothing wrong. In fact, every male on our volunteer team struggled with pornography, and they were not being treated differently by people in the church. All Dan did was follow what Scripture asks of us—he confessed. He confessed and he trusted he would be dealt with in Christlike love. Instead, bad ideas, bad practice, and ungodly barriers deeply wounded my friend Dan. After my initial meeting with Dan I wondered if I might be ready to share my own experience, but the backlash only pushed me further into the closet. Dan and I have not spoken in years. I know he has rejected his faith, left his wife and kid for a string of male sexual encounters, and spends a lot of energy on social media enunciating his hatred of the church.

What happened to my friend Dan, and what would later happen to me, is tame compared to the devastating harm other same-sex-attracted and LGBTQ+ people have endured in the church. More and more mental health professionals are sounding the alarm that LGBTQ+ youth growing up in nonaccepting religious spaces can experience devastating-long term psychological effects.[2]

You don't have to look too far back to see that the church has historically had a contentious relationship with the LGBTQ+ community. You barely have to look over your shoulder. In many contexts, the posture of Christians toward our LGBTQ+ neighbors has been caustic at best and dangerously violent at worst.

In Eugene, Oregon, near where I grew up, there is a high population of homeless youth, many of whom identify somewhere within the LGBTQ+ community. And many of them were kicked out of their homes by parents with Bibles in their hands.[3] Historically in America, LGTBQ+ people have experienced verbal abuse, physical assault, or ostracism from family, friends, work, and church. Even today many people will not tolerate the existence of LGBTQ+ people.

Bigotry and violence, while always reprehensible, should not catch us off guard. Ever since Cain murdered Abel people have experienced an "us vs. them" dynamic that appeals to our worst impulses. We have always feared, rejected, or despised those we view as "other." This wickedness is as old as our species. But what should surprise us, and devastate us, is how often hatred and violence have come from the hands of Christians.

And so in church, sometimes LGBTQ+ people have to hide to be loved. Bridgette Eileen Rivera writes, "No matter what queer people do, how they live, how they talk, or how they define their own existence, when many Christians meet an LGBTQ+ person they see a pathological sinner. A pervert. All people sin, but LGBTQ+ people are sinners without grace."[4]

No one should have to leave church in order to find healing. Churches are supposed to be houses of healing, where broken people go to get better through the love of our Great Physician. We should never feel a moral quandary about inviting someone, anyone, to church because of the psychological and spiritual harm we may be exposing them to. These are not acceptable scenarios for the body of Christ.

As my friend Preston Sprinkle often says, "Churches are supposed to be a hospital for the spiritually sick, so when did they become a graveyard for LGBTQ+ people?"

REJECTING FIG LEAVES

Feeling like we must hide pieces of ourselves in order to be loved is not only an LGBTQ+ thing, it's a human thing. Hiding is how we have learned to deal with the less-than-desirable parts of ourselves. It is an instinct that can be traced back to our first ancestors, Adam and Eve.

Genesis 3 recounts the story this way:

> The woman saw that the tree was good for food and delightful to look at, and that it was desirable for obtaining wisdom. So she took some of its fruit and ate it; she also gave some to her husband, who was with her, and he ate it.

> Then the eyes of both of them were opened, and they knew they were naked; so they sewed fig leaves together and made coverings for themselves. (Genesis 3:6-7 CSB)

The moment Adam and Eve's eyes were opened, their first response was not wonder but shame. They reached for fig leaves, desperate to cover what they feared could no longer be seen without judgment. And we've been sewing fig leaves ever since.

We may not use leaves and branches, but we become just as skilled in crafting coverings—masks of competence, curated images, half-truths about who we are and what we struggle with. We convince ourselves that only the polished version of us is lovable. But the tragedy of hiding is that it keeps us from the very thing we long for most: to be fully known and fully loved.

The gospel is God's refusal to let us keep hiding. In Jesus, God comes walking into our shame like he once walked into the garden, asking not "What have you done?" but "Where are you?" He is not searching for perfection but for presence. He doesn't want the mask, the cover-up, the curated self. God is not interested in who you're pretending to be, he wants you. The cross is God's ultimate declaration that he sees it all and still chooses to love. This is God's heart for all people, including our LGBTQ+ neighbors. As M. Robert Mullholland expertly put it, "The unfathomable depths of our belovedness is revealed in the cruciform love of God in Christ. . . . The cruciform love of God, which plumbs the depths of our unholiness, is, at the same time, the sanctifying love of God."[5]

REFLECTION QUESTIONS

1. Do you know what it feels like to hide to be loved? What has that looked like for you?
2. In your faith community or family, do you think LGBTQ+ people might feel an inordinate pressure to hide? Why or why not?
3. How do you imagine it makes God feel to see LGBTQ+ being treated differently than other sinners and saints in church?

3

THE HISTORY OF HARM

When I became a Christian, I thought I could trust the Church to behave like Christ. But I found that often the institution, like any other human one, gets in the way of the Gospel rather than spreading it.

C. S. Lewis

When I pastored Open Table Church, I would lead our church in the Apostles Creed. I would recite the same preamble every week, explaining why we recited the creed: "The story we live in is the story we live out. The stories we believe about the world shape how we live in the world. So every week we recite the Apostles Creed as a way of reminding followers of Jesus what story we believe about the world."

Human beings are storied creatures. We tell stories to make meaning of reality. Whether atheist, fundamentalist Christian, or spiritual-but-not-religious sojourner, there is not a person alive who hasn't bought into some story to make sense of the world.

When things happen to us in our lives that are out of our control, our brains seem to automatically form a story around these events. These stories are full of detail and feeling. This is why it is not uncommon for kids to feel at fault when their parents divorce. They have formulated a story to make sense of their pain. The stories we believe about the world shape our core beliefs, and our core beliefs color how we think about, feel, and interpret everything.

To enter into loving union with Jesus and into community with the church is, ultimately, to enter into a story. Followers of Jesus have a story of being created with purpose, intention, and immeasurable value. We have a story to explain the chaos, frailty, and evil both in the world and in our own hearts. And we have a story that offers redemption, beauty, restoration, peace, and reconciliation with God and one another.

LGBTQ+ people in church are often offered a different story. For us, it is often communicated (implicitly or explicitly) that we are prime examples of the fall and the least likely to receive the redemption. This story colors everything we believe about God, church, and ourselves. It is an untrue, harmful, and all-too-common story.

GLORIA AND ADAM

I was fourteen years old when my youth group took a trip to a city just a couple of hours away from my hometown. As part of our trip we spent a day helping out at a homeless shelter downtown. After we were done serving, one of the leaders whipped out his guitar and started singing worship songs. This would seem a little bizarre today, but it was very common at the time. Youth group worship leaders in the mid-2000s were eager to brandish their guitars and start singing "How Great Is Our God" at the most random times. A few of the volunteers and the transient people joined us.

After the second song, a lady looking to be in her mid-fifties started yelling at us to stop. Actually, "yelling" is putting it too mildly. She was full-on screaming. She looked dirty and her clothes were ragged, and our sheltered little youth group got really quiet really quick. God was great, but he was going to have to wait to hear us sing about it.

At first I was offended. Given my narrowly fundamentalist upbringing, I wondered if a demon in her was tormented by our praise. Or maybe she was on some drug. But when I looked at her I saw tears streaming down her face. She didn't look angry or possessed or high, she looked like she was in grief. The leaders asked her what her name was.

"Gloria," she told us.

Then they asked her what was wrong.

"I can't listen to music like that!" she shouted. "It pretends to be all about love but it is so hateful."

Gloria proceeded to tell us about her son, Adam. Gloria and her husband had raised Adam in a deeply conservative Christian home. But when Adam was thirteen years old he came out to his parents as gay. She went on to tell us they tried everything they could to "cure" him of his homosexuality.

"I never thought there was anything wrong with my baby, but I knew he was going to be eaten alive by his father and our church if he didn't find a way to change," she said.

She explained how they'd sent him to a special camp that was intended to heal his homosexuality. They held prayer meetings in their living room, having the church elders lay hands on him and pray for deliverance. As he entered high school they tried setting Adam up on dates with different girls from youth group or school. At one point Adam's father even showed him heterosexual pornography to try to prove to his son that he could be aroused by heterosexual sex (apparently, pornography was a much more acceptable sin). Nothing worked.

Eventually, their pastor told Gloria and her husband that Adam was being willfully rebellious, that he was choosing not to renounce his homosexuality. They were advised to kick Adam out of their house and to welcome him back only if he sincerely repented of his homosexuality. Gloria believed her son was doing his best, but her husband followed the pastor's advice.

Adam was sent to live on the street when he was sixteen. Family members and friends from church were instructed to treat Adam like a drug addict in need of tough love. Gloria told us that her husband would say things like, "If he calls looking for a place to sleep, do not help him unless he tells you he's ready to repent. He needs to hit rock bottom. If we let him receive help before he repents, he will never get better."

Eventually Adam found community among the homeless youth on the streets of Portland. Soon he did become an addict. After two years of addiction and homelessness, when Adam was eighteen, he broke into his parents' house and hung himself from the rafters in their garage.

Gloria found him.

This mother told us her story with tears streaming down her face. Her only begotten son had hung on a wooden beam because of the sins inflicted upon him. Judgment triumphed over mercy.

A tragedy that gave her more in common with God than most of us will ever face led Gloria to atheism, divorce, her own addiction issues, and homelessness.

When she recognized the song our worship leader was singing from her old church, the pain was too much. It was this pain that prompted her to beg us to stop. And it was the first time in my life I thought not singing worship songs was the right thing to do.

Our youth group stayed in the gymnasium of a church that night. *Is this the same church Gloria and Adam went to?* I wondered. Probably not. I lay on the floor in my blue and gray sleeping bag, headphones in, Green Day's *American Idiot* playing on my portable CD player. I stared up at the rafters thinking about Adam's devastating end.

This encounter took place shortly after I realized my own same-sex attraction. That year my mind was flooded with thoughts of suicide. And I wondered if my own story was doomed to end like Adam's.

The story we live in is the story we live out. Adam lived in a story that told him these aspects of himself—aspects he had no say over—marked him as indefensibly vile. His story taught him that he was not worth being loved by the people who were supposed to love him most. Gloria lived in a story that taught her Christianity was true and good only to later find out that it was actually a distributor of pain and chaos. As I lay on that floor, I told myself a story to make sense of the chaotic world I found myself in.

IN CHURCH AND IN THE CLOSET

I want to invite you on a journey with me back to the year 2004. This was the year *Friends*, the greatest sitcom of all time, came to an end. This was the year Disney's superfamily *The Incredibles* hit theaters. This was back when Donald Trump firing somebody was just a fun thing he did on TV and not a cause for global news.[1]

It was also the year I realized I wasn't straight.

I'd had inklings before that year that something was different about me. Strange dreams, bewildering feelings, confusing relational dynamics. But I hadn't discovered anything concrete. Then came church camp that August, and I bunked in a room full of boys my age. The camp was short-staffed so we did not have a counselor in our room. Locking a group of puberty-struck middle school boys in a room without any adult supervision—what could possibly go wrong?

I was bunking with a boy I'd experienced confusing feelings toward. As the camp went on, one thing led to another, and I shared my first sexual experience with him. This conservative, homeschooled, Pentecostal boy's first sexual experience was with another boy, and it was at church camp of all places. It sounds like an episode of *South Park* but it's true.

After this other boy and I were done, a blanket of shame, grief, and terror fell on me. I went into the bathroom and wept as quietly as I could. I wept because I did not know I was capable of doing what I had just done; I wept because I felt powerless over the situation. I knew going forward there was no mystery to my peculiar feelings. I had opened a door that would not be shut. And I was convinced I would spend the rest of my life trying to prove to God and my family that I was still worth loving and embracing.

I wept because *I* believed I was no longer worth loving.

This moment at age twelve would mark an eleven-year journey of shame, hiding, depression, suicidality, and the deepest fear I had ever known. Twenty years later I am still working through the deeply ingrained pain wreaked on me by this shame.

In my church, and among certain members of my family, it was not uncommon for our LGBTQ+ neighbors to be talked about in the same terms as pedophiles and people who have sex with animals. This was not something they taught us in children's Sunday school, thankfully. But while people were mingling in the hallways before and after services, or when we'd have church socials, or at gatherings with extended family, cruel language around this topic was not uncommon.

You see, another pivotal moment in 2004 was Massachusetts becoming the first state to legalize gay marriage. In response, evangelical faith communities across the country went into in full-blown panic about how "the gay agenda" was going to sweep across the country and debase our youth.

This was the beginning of a tectonic shift in our country. Up until that point superstar evangelical leaders had been enjoying their status as prominent power brokers in society. Cultural power is often maintained by fearmongering, waging one culture war after another in one's constituency, because fear is the most effective way to rally people around your cause. In the United States, these powerful individuals spread anxiety by heralding the loss of our identity as a "Christian nation." This is a national identity I've come to believe never actually existed. But Massachusetts's decision to legalize gay marriage was a sign evangelical leaders were losing their influence in significant parts of the country. So they sounded the alarm.

A few sweet, well-meaning older ladies in my church were some of the biggest crusaders when it came to spreading this anxiety. Before my experience at church camp I'd thought these ladies were sweet, affectionate, and tender. And they were all of those things. But after camp I felt only one thing around them—fear.

As I continued past the eighth grade and puberty reached the height of its tyrannical reign in my body, my desires for certain people of the same sex grew more difficult to ignore. So did my fear. Just seeing these older ladies at church caused anxiety to jolt through my body. Hearing Gloria and Adam's story added fuel to the fire. I was convinced these women would urge my parents to do to me what Gloria's pastor had told her to do to Adam: Kick me out and withhold their love from me.

Before I knew I wasn't straight, the story I believed about God was that he was kind and good, and the story I believed about myself was that I was loved by God. I never doubted that in my family I was safe and cherished. But after realizing I wasn't heterosexual, after observing how Christians talked and thought about LGBTQ+ people, those gentle stories were replaced with harsher ones. God was no longer loving and family was no longer safe. Going to church made me feel more alienated from God and people than reconciled to them.

If anyone found out my secret, life as I knew it would be over. I was convinced I would lose my family, friends, and church and be treated like a monster. I also feared that being found out would open the door to additional sexual experiences. I was scared that if certain opportunities presented themselves, I would not be able to resist.

UNWANTED DESIRES AND SUFFOCATING MESSAGES

The idea of unwanted desires is wrapped up in a mystifying tension, especially when it comes to the intersection of faith and sexuality. Unwanted desires are things we want that we don't want to want. Anyone immersed in Christianity who has wrestled with same-sex desires or an incongruence between the biological self and the internal self will understand this. Our bodies and their urges feel hardwired to lean one way, but the convictions of our faith demand we resist.

We genuinely want intimacy and romantic connection with people of the same sex. We also loath that we want those things and would give anything to rid ourselves of these desires, because we see the truth and beauty of the Bible's vision of sex and marriage. Transgender people may read about God creating humans as gendered beings and understand that their bodies are not just biological but theological, and they may still feel like their internal self was placed in the wrong body. Tragically, this can lead to feeling like the real them has been buried alive and is slowly suffocating until they become what is functionally a walking corpse.

The task, I am learning, is to become someone who embraces my whole story without burying key aspects of myself. I strive to do this without allowing those things to compromise my fidelity to the way of Jesus and the Scriptures. It's an enormous task. With so few public models and the absence of teaching on how to do it, the process can often feel excruciating.

Hopefully over time the person who experiences these desires or dysphoria learns to see themselves the way their Father in heaven sees them, with eyes of love. Once we are seen with the eyes of love, once we see that our bodies and identities have been handcrafted from our Creator with purpose, love, and intention, we can trust our Creator's vision of holy living. We not only trust it, but flourish more than ever.

But if we dwell in a community that teaches we are inherently gross and irredeemable due to pieces of ourselves we did not choose and cannot shake, the self-hatred can be acute and crippling. These competing longings—or, to quote David Bennet, this "war of loves"—can be an impossibly heavy burden to bear.[2] Add to the equation the shame-inducing components of silence, secrecy, and judgment, and the LGTBQ+ person in the pew is primed for a breakdown.

One of the most-repeated encouragements found in the pages of Scripture is some variation of "fear not" or "have courage." Moses told the Israelites not to panic or be afraid right before his death (Deuteronomy 31:6-8). The Lord told Joshua to be strong and courageous before entering the Promised Land (Joshua 1:9). The great prophet Isaiah proclaimed to Israel that they need not fear the coming judgment for God was their help (Isaiah 41:14). Jesus told his disciples not to let their hearts be troubled or afraid (John 14:27). Paul instructed his young protégé Timothy that God had not given him a spirit of fear but of power, love, and self-discipline (2 Timothy 1:7). We would be hard-pressed to read a book of the Bible without being told repeatedly that with a God this good, this loving, this merciful, and this powerful, we do not need to fear.

And yet God's call to "fear not" felt incompatible with my experience of the God-followers who also spoke so cruelly about people like me. Church had become a place of perpetual fear for me. I was afraid of being rejected. I was afraid the televangelists and conservative news pundits were right, that I was a deplorable abomination. I wanted nothing more than to tell someone my whole story and be received with love and safety, but telling someone appeared to be life-threatening. I was afraid of my unwanted sexual desires, because try as I might, I could not control what I wanted. And it terrified me that I wanted these things.

What does this say about me? I often wondered. Were my desires a sign that I was more broken, abominable, and depraved than people who didn't experience these desires? What did this say about God? Did he really make me just to condemn me?

The scariest things in the world to me weren't ghosts, monsters, boogeymen, or even other gay people. I was most afraid of the church lady who could make cookies and give warm hugs one moment and plunge into a vitriolic, impassioned, homophobic tirade the next.

I saw how LGBTQ+ people were treated by Christians and the tragic direction their lives took. I heard how we were talked about from the pulpit, in church hallways, on Fox News, at dinner tables, and while hanging out with friends. We were the enemy, the thing that threatened to steal the soul of America and compromise the holiness of the church. We were little better than child predators. We were gross, unnatural, the butt of the joke, too effeminate or too masculine. Grown men would speak fearfully and violently about the prospect of being hit on by other men, as if the only gender deserving of unwanted male attention was female. We were fags, homos, dykes, and trannies.

Nobody in my circle knew that when they expressed their disdain for LGBTQ+ people they were talking about me. These conversations shaped my view of who I was, who God was, and what was most important in life. They became the story I lived in and the story I lived out.

And so, over the years, as I grew into a young man on the outside, on the inside I remained a terrified, lonely kid convinced he was unworthy of love and belonging. To protect myself I grew aggressive, violent, sexually impulsive, and prone to escapism via a good party, a good road trip, a good movie, or (gulp) endless hours on MySpace.

Eventually this fear, shame, hiding, and deep self-hatred led me to the conclusion that I did not want to live anymore. I survived one suicide attempt and a near-attempt that involved my father's revolver. My arms bear scars from the cuts I inflicted on myself whenever I lusted after a guy. When I was sixteen years old I carved the word *FAIL* into the skin of my left forearm after holding hands with a boy while watching a movie. We didn't have sex, kiss, or cuddle. We held hands and I was elated. Afterward, so ashamed I needed to find a way to punish myself, I cut *FAIL*. The scar still has not totally faded.

In high school I would pick fights over the most ridiculous things as a way to assert my masculinity. Sure, I may have preferred theater over football, and sure, I liked the *Wicked* soundtrack more than I liked the Red-Hot Chili Peppers. But if I could beat you in a fight, you'd think twice about questioning my sexuality or manhood.

INNER DISSONANCE

When I reflect on my adolescent years I am forced to ask a number of uncomfortable questions. Why was I—someone who grew up in the church, who went to church camp every year, who had two loving parents, who was part of a great community, who genuinely loved Jesus and wanted to do right by him—such a dysfunctional kid?

Why did I feel safer with my agnostic friends than I did with my church friends? Why was my choir teacher more comforting than my youth pastor? Why did I have friends who would never darken the doorway of a church door but who I knew would love and accept me if they knew my secret? Why couldn't I go to church without hyperventilating because I was afraid I would "out myself" by sounding too effeminate if I talked?

And here's the question that keeps me up at night: If I had not been part of the church when I realized I wasn't straight, would I have still hated myself as much as I did, for as long as I did? Would I have become addicted to self-harm? Would I have picked so many fights? Would I now have a scar spelling *FAIL* on my arm? Would I have come so close to killing myself twice?

The church has given me the things I value most in the world: my relationship with Jesus and devotion to living out his way. I met the girl of my dreams, my wife, Kelsey, through a friend from church. My calling to be a pastor and the unmatched joy and meaning that brings me came from, and can exist only in, the church. My closest friends and the level of commitment and intimacy I experience with them were birthed out of the church. My love of teaching others about Jesus, my passion for Scripture, theology, church history, and emotionally healthy spirituality—all of these things are core to who I am.

The most pivotal pieces of myself were shaped by the church. But some of the most painful, traumatizing, agonizing moments of my life were given to me by Christians. These Christians sincerely meant well but did not know how to love someone with my particular struggles. These Christians hurt me without knowing they were hurting me.

Why was this issue, this struggle that was the unpardonable evil, worthy of inflicting so much shame? Why did I hate myself when I fantasized over boys but not when I lied to my parents? Why did I desire to kill myself when I developed romantic attraction to boys but not when I stole an Eminem CD from Walmart? Why did I feel pride, not shame, when I managed to have sexual encounters with girls but thought I was in league with Satan when I held a boy's hand?

I think it's because the barriers for people who struggle with this issue in the church are different from those for people who struggle with other issues. Growing up in church I saw men and women held in high regard who were judgmental, dishonest, gossipy, divorced, and greedy, as well as folks who could not get themselves to stop watching pornography. I knew of pastors who sacrificed their families on the altar of ministry and elders who were divorced and remarried. At the churches I grew up in, or those I visited with friends, I saw room for all types of people. Room for grace, redemption, calling, being asked to contribute and lead. There was room for all types of people except one. There was no one who openly struggled with their sexual orientation. We rarely talked about the issue from our pulpits, but when we did—yikes.

I grew up in church thinking it was much easier for Jesus to love greedy business owners, cons, addicts, overhurried pastors, and judgmental church ladies than it was for Jesus to love me. Although I have attended church my whole life and been in ministry for nearly fifteen years, I am still anxious every time I step foot inside a church building.

Even when I am invited to speak at a church about the exact things I'm writing about in this book, I have to pause and pray before I go in. I have an almost primal distrust of religious leaders and spaces. Every time I go to a church, which is where I spend most of my time, I have to overcome fear.

It should not be that way, and it doesn't have to be that way for incoming generations of Jesus-followers.

VIOLENT MESSAGES PAST AND PRESENT

In the 1970s, Florida's Key West was quite the hub for vacationing gay men. Their presence, flamboyance, and parties were not welcomed by many Key West locals. These men were referred to as invaders, screamed at, spat on, and attacked. One pastor, Rev. Morris Wright, was so disgusted by their presence he decided to take matters into his own hands.

Reverend Wright placed an advertisement in the *Key West Citizen* in which he wrote, "If I were the chief of police I would get me a hundred good men, give them each a baseball bat and have them walk down Duval Street and dare one of these freaks to stick his head over the edge of the sidewalk. . . . That is the way it was done in Key West in the days I remember and loved. Female impersonators and queers were loaded into a deputy's automobile and shipped to the county line."[3]

For Reverend Wright, gay and trans people belonged in prison or the grave. And he is not the only faith leader who has expressed these kinds of sentiments. Pastor Dillon Awes made headlines for his comments from the pulpit of Steadfast Baptist Church in Watauga, Texas. He told his congregation that gay people "are dangerous to society. . . . All homosexuals are pedophiles . . . and should be shot in the head."[4] And lest you think these are the antiquated musings of some homophobic televangelist from the 1970s, Awes made these comments in 2022.

Now, if you are reading this book, you are likely a follower of Jesus and likely appalled by Awes's statements. You are also not likely to be attending a church where you are going to hear something like that from the pulpit. I am also willing to wager that you don't know very many, if any, professing Christians who would support Pastor Dillon's egregious remarks. However, you also know as well as I do how easily perception masquerades as reality.

Every time a Christian leader like Pastor Dillon makes headlines for remarks like this, a story is being told, a story that sends a loud-and-clear message that Christians are bigoted, homophobic, and dangerous. And these claims are not always baseless.

In the year 2000, Ronald Gay entered the Backstreet Café, a gay bar, and opened fire, killing one person and injuring six others. He claimed that God had instructed him to target LGBTQ+ individuals, describing himself as a "Christian soldier working for my Lord."[5]

Consider how evangelicals responded to the AIDS crisis in the eighties and nineties. While a generation was dying from a horrific disease in agonizing ways, many Christians took the opportunity to announce God's judgment on the community.[6] To be sure, several Christians responded in love and generosity, but few of them made the news, and even fewer identified as evangelical.[7] Sadly, the witness of the church in that time was often one of finger waving, condemnation, and a smug self-righteousness.

In 1981, godfather of conservative American evangelicalism Jerry Falwell gave a talk on his radio broadcast describing gay people as an infestation bringing about the moral decay of America. He spoke of militant gays trying to silence him, warned of "homosexual recruiting tactics," and promised (as long as he was supported by donations) to continue to lead the charge against this "satanic homosexual revolution."[8] In the mid-1980s Falwell famously told fellow faith leader Francis Schaeffer, "If I had a dog who did what they did, I'd shoot it."[9]

Falwell was a formative figure. He spearheaded what is now known as the Moral Majority and did much to tangle Christianity with right-wing politics. He was a type of kingmaker, using his influence to help elect men like Ronald Reagan, George Bush, and George W. Bush. His son, Jerry Falwell Jr., was instrumental in Donald Trump's successful bid for president in 2016. The elder Falwell also founded Liberty University, one of the largest Christian colleges in the world.

All to say that Jerry Falwell, while less tactful than many Christians today would prefer, was not a fringe player in American church history. His influence on much of American evangelicalism runs deep even still, and he regularly painted the LGBTQ+ community as dangerous and devious—vagrants who, if tolerated, would corrupt the soul of our churches and America as a whole.

Falwell's words show that he did not see human beings made in the image of God when he looked at gay or trans people, at least according to his public statements. He saw the enemy, pawns of Satan, an ideology that scared him. While modern evangelicalism is in a bit of an identity crisis these days, the influence of Jerry Falwell still looms large over American Christianity.[10]

THE PROBLEM PERSISTS TODAY

Falwell is not an outlier. His words represent what many in the American church considered common-sense thinking about the LGBTQ+ community at the time. While it might be easy to say, "That was twenty to forty years ago; we have come so far since then," I am concerned that this aggressive posture of the church toward LGBTQ+ people has not gone away. It has merely adopted different forms.

Today the barriers LGBTQ+ people face in the church are subtler than they used to be. Nonetheless, they keep sincere queer people who are curious about Christ and the church at bay. Today, in numerous faith communities across the West, if we were to dig beneath the surface of the automated smiles and brief handshakes that take place on an average Sunday, I'm convinced we would find the remaining root system of Falwell's beliefs about gay and trans people.

Can you believe there are LGBTQ+ people who still want to go to church? If you were a person who identified somewhere in the LGBTQ+ community, would *you* want to go to church? More specifically, would you want to go to *your* church? If you were a queer person, how would you feel about attending your family or social gatherings? Think about that for a moment.

If you were an LGBTQ+ person and you saw how Christians spoke about or behaved toward people like you, would you feel safe to go to church, or even a desire to do so? Many straight people have a hard time answering that question in the affirmative.

If people leave church or faith because the call to carry a cross is too much, or because they can't get themselves to believe in God, let alone God incarnate as a Jewish carpenter-rabbi who died and was resurrected two thousand years ago, or because they simply will not abide by the ethical teachings of Scripture, then so be it. I wish they wouldn't, but those are all right and valid reasons for someone to avoid church. But if people reject the church because they find it unempathetic, capricious, unkind, unloving, cruel, fearful, theologically lazy, relationally rigid, closed-minded, or just plain ignorant, well, that's a blight on the church, not the person leaving it.

Church is full of people who are just doing their best to limp their way toward Christlikeness. Every church I've been a part of has had a place for people with different limps. Alcoholics, gambling addicts, cheaters, drug addicts, porn addicts, racists, hypocrites, and more. But there was not space for people who experienced attraction to the same sex or struggled with their gender identity. Sure, we could come to church and maybe even fit in as long as we hid our limp, but we could never belong. True belonging requires us to be received with our whole stories in scope. Fitting in is a cheap substitute for belonging.

A MORE CHRISTLIKE FAITH

For any honest student of the Gospels, it is difficult to square the history of harm we covered with the Christ revealed in Scripture. Much of this harm is incongruent with the teachings and example of Jesus. This is not a trivial matter. In their exceptional book *Slow Theology*, Drs. A. J. Swoboda and Nijay Gupta write, "The aim of Christian theology is the adoration of the God who was revealed as a real human with a real name—Jesus Christ. Christian theology must always be harnessed to the history of this particular person and must seek to follow him in all things."[11]

To practice Christianity in a harmful manner is theological compromise. If we are harnessing our theology toward the person of Jesus, the fruit of this will be shalom, not the shattering of shalom. To practice Christianity ought to be synonymous with practicing the way of Jesus. Any version of Christianity that propagates un-Christlike attitudes and behaviors is in need of substantial renovation. Much of what is required to care for our LGBTQ+ neighbors starts with examining the Christlikeness of our theology and practice.

REFLECTION QUESTIONS

1. What thoughts and feelings did you notice come up in you as you read some of these stories?
2. Why do you suspect stories like these, past and present, have been tolerated in the church?
3. What stories of harm toward LGBTQ+ have you seen or heard?

4

CASUALTIES OF CULTURE WAR

As to all opinions that do not strike to the root of Christianity, we think and let think.

John Wesley

With my family's deep roots in American Pentecostalism, one name I have known for as long as I've known any name is Jimmy Swaggart. Now, my family was only nominally interested in this Baton Rouge–born televangelist. My mom's side of the family cared more than my dad, as my dad, who became a Christian as an adult, didn't much care for the evangelical subculture. By the time I came along, Swaggart was mostly a juicy conversation topic, as public scandal brought about his very public downfall. After his fall from grace he was defrocked by his denomination, but over the next few decades he rebuilt some of what he'd lost. By 2004 he was pastoring a local church again, with a sanctuary that held over seven hundred people. His preaching went on the radio, television, the internet, and was broadcast all over the world.

In 2004, the first gay marriage in American history occurred, and the Defense of Marriage Act (a bill that would prevent same-sex marriages) was being hotly debated. Many evangelicals were fiercely engaged in the battle to define marriage for American citizens, and anxiety surrounding the issue was high. Just three years earlier, evangelical celebrities Jerry Falwell and Pat Robertson had said on *The 700 Club* that 9/11 was an act of God's judgment on America, in part because of "the gays."[1]

For me, the summer of 2004 was also the time when my suspicions about my sexuality were all but confirmed and I resolved never to tell anyone (see how well that worked out?). That September I remember reading *To Kill a Mockingbird* in the living room with my dad while he was watching television. Even though we were in the same room, my secret made me feel as though we were living on different planets.

My dad's channel surfing stopped on the infamous Baton Rouge preacher. Swaggart was fired up. He was sweating and waving his Bible around. His communication style was hard to look away from. And he said something in that sermon I'll never forget: "We need a constitutional amendment that states that marriage is between a man and a woman. . . . This utter, absolute asinine, idiotic stupidity of men marrying men . . . I've never seen a man in my life I wanted to marry. And I'm gonna be blunt and plain: If one ever looks at me like that, I'm gonna kill him and tell God he died."[2]

The message was clear. Being gay was so obscene, so unnatural, so disgusting, that if a God-fearing man caught even a hint of attraction from another man, he ought to be so grossed out it could become violent. Swaggart's words in that cultural moment had me quietly dismissing myself to my bedroom in tears.

Swaggart later clarified that the comment was intended to be a lighthearted joke and apologized to anyone he had offended. But the damage had been done. His violent words communicated that Christians were literally at war with gay people. And because of messaging like this, many Christians felt immense pressure to engage in this culture war. Their anxieties and fears were stoked by politicians and televangelists to take up arms against anyone who was an ideological enemy.

Christians face a similar anxious tension today in the hot debates around gender transitioning, especially for minors. There is nothing new under the sun. For decades, LGBTQ+ people have found themselves at the center of Christian culture wars. And for decades, this has done untold damage to the Christian witness.

QUICK TO THE DRAW

The political issues Christians tend to get fired up about should not be ignored. They matter. Marriage, the sanctity of life, whether teens should have access to permanently life-altering hormones and surgeries—these are weighty, significant matters. The fact that it is legal in many states for minors to have healthy parts of their body removed before they can get a tattoo, smoke, drink, or join the military is a rational thing to be outraged by. So do not misunderstand me when I say I am wary about how quick to the draw Christians are in culture wars. It's not that I think these things don't matter. They certainly do. But culture-warring Christianity almost always has two dangerous side effects.

First, culture wars make Christian hypocrisy dangerously easy. An exhaustive emphasis on one topic tends to make us blind to others. We try hard to violently remove specks from other people's eyeballs and fail to do so because we've got massive logs in our own. This 2004 sermon from Jimmy Swaggart was nowhere near the first time he'd behaved aggressively in the pulpit. Attacking, mocking, and lambasting sinners had been his trademark preaching style for decades. And all the while he was in his own private battle with disordered, sinful behavior.

While our platforms may be less public than Swaggart's, many Christians in culture wars become similarly obsessed with others' sin and blind to their own. It's hard to engage in culture wars without becoming hypocrites. Consider the very term "culture war." The implication is that there is a war for control of the culture, and as in all wars, enemies must be eliminated. We cannot engage in any type of war, including culture wars, without being dominated by the fear of losing. When fear is running the show, love is subdued. When love is subdued, we lose a grasp on the beautiful aims of the gospel. If we want to stand a chance of reaching people alienated from God, particularly LGBTQ+ people, we have to do away with things that compromise our witness.

A culture war inevitably invites an overfocus on one issue, which may or may not actually be a kingdom issue, and causes us to underfocus on other issues. As such, much of the Western church is marred with a hypocritical reputation. While we target our energy by lambasting trans people and postmodern gender theory, we overlook our own worship of money, power, and success. While we rail against gay marriage, we overlook the fact that divorce in the church isn't much less common than divorce outside the church.

The second side effect of culture-warring Christianity is that it fundamentally shifts our identity away from the one Christ gave us. Our focus changes from being reconcilers of heaven and earth to being domineering power brokers in the culture. A recent documentary series, *Shiny Happy People; A Teenage Holy War*, covers the ministry of Teen Mania founder Ron Luce, giving attention to his Acquire the Fire and BattleCry conferences. The series sheds light on Luce's use of military imagery, violent language, and conditioning of children to believe they were the Navy SEALs of God's kingdom. Luce, along with other prominent evangelicals like James Dobson and Jerry Falwell, used aggressive and borderline brainwashing tactics to shape children into seeing themselves primarily as culture warriors.[3]

If being a Christian means being a follower of Jesus, being his apprentice, that means our calling is to take on his yoke (Matthew 11:29). *Yoke* is an ancient idiom meaning we are to take on Jesus' way of life as our way of life. Jesus did not approach life as someone at war with the culture, and he didn't commission his disciples to "go into all the world and win arguments, offend intentionally, and spread anxiety." Christ lived a life that invited alienated people into reconciliation with God. Christ bore witness to the goodness, beauty, and truth of his kingdom. His students and followers are called to do likewise.

We are called not to take on the yoke of politicians or influential pastors but to take on the yoke of Jesus. As Dallas Willard wrote, we need to have an "intelligent, informed, unyielding resolve to live as Jesus lived in all aspects of life."[4] Culture wars, with their aggression, fear, and anxiety, can't help but eclipse this sacred calling.

A BAD WITNESS

It is important to acknowledge the distinction between the culture-warring often seen in segments of modern Christianity and the holy activism embodied by figures such as Martin Luther King Jr. or William Wilberforce. Culture-warring tends to be reactive, fear-driven, and obsessed with symbolic battles—protesting drag queen story hours or fixating on the perceived erosion of family values. This posture is often less concerned with love of neighbor or systemic justice and more with preserving a sense of cultural dominance. It trades the cross for the megaphone, opting to stir up anxiety and outrage rather than doing the quiet, costly work of sacrificial love. In this mode, enemies are to be exposed, defeated, and driven out—not prayed for, reasoned with, or won over through compassion.

By contrast, the activism of King and Wilberforce was deeply rooted in the character of Christ and the long arc of redemptive history. Their work was driven not by fear of cultural loss but by a vision of God's justice breaking into human affairs. Wilberforce labored patiently for decades to dismantle the transatlantic slave trade, not because he wanted to "win" a culture war but because he was compelled by the gospel to stand with the oppressed. King's civil rights activism, likewise, was not a reaction to secularization but a prophetic call to embody the kingdom of God in public life. Both men saw justice not as a weapon to wield but as a burden to carry—anchored in love, animated by hope, and oriented toward reconciliation. Where culture-warring divides, holy activism heals. Where culture-warring seeks victory, holy activism seeks the shalom of God.

Next to the history of harm, culture wars are the biggest deterrent keeping spiritually curious LGBTQ+ people out of church. Until we understand the reactivity behind our impulse to pick a fight, we can't hope to choose peacemaking over warmongering. Faithful Christian discipleship is not possible without a robust peacemaking instinct. And effective ministry to LGBTQ+ people is hindered by anxious and outraged Christianity.

If culture-warring has been so harmful to the Christian witness, why are many Christians so eager to engage with it? There are three reasons worth examining: disorientation brought on by the changing tides of culture, misplaced identity, and cycles of anxiety. We'll look at changing tides in this chapter and the others in the next.

Changing cultural tides manifest primarily in three ways: as political shifts, spiritual shifts, and shifts in power dynamics. Any of these shifts can be a catalyst for Christian engagement in culture war. They also help us understand why conversations in the church about our LGBTQ+ neighbors are often riddled with anxiety and suspicion.

POLITICAL SHIFT

We live in a moment of unprecedented change. The speed of change has accelerated and intensified more in the last thirty years than at any other point in human history.[5] The consciousness-changing innovation of the internet, and the all-encompassing power of carrying the internet around in our pockets and purses, has wrought a speed of change so severe we do not have time to assess the impact of it all.

We can see the impact of this change in everything from technology to philosophy, from how we make movies to how we watch them, from how we order our food to how we pay for it, from the decline of belief in objective truth to the rise of passionate and objective activism, from our sexual ethics to our understanding of the human body.

Everything is changing. And on an existential, psychological, and spiritual level, this unprecedented speed of change comes at a cost. Renowned therapist and leadership consultant Edwin Friedman described the cost of living in such a rapidly changing society. He writes, "An entire society could lose its ability to cope with change. . . . Anxiety escalates as a society is overwhelmed by the quantity and speed of change."[6]

In the United States specifically, we see how this rapid change invokes anxiety, and this anxiety is being expressed in our politics. Now, I am not here to belittle people who are afraid. The things people fear in regard to politics and LGBTQ+ issues make sense to me, even if I think fear is a fundamentally unchristian motivator.[7] Ultimately, what many Christians are afraid of is loved ones walking away from their faith, rejecting Christian orthodoxy, and suffering consequences for it. They are afraid of what a life out of union with Christ will bring for their loved ones. They are afraid of what others will think of them, especially within the church.

I have sat with too many parents who are watching their teenagers make irreversible choices about their bodies as they transition to tell you the politics around this are not daunting. I have seen too many people lose relationships with their friends, children, and even their spouses as it has become more culturally acceptable to embrace a queer identity. I have seen too much pain to say this fear is totally unfounded, even if fear does fall short of God's standard. These things cause pain, and we fear things that cause pain. That is natural.

The fear we feel in changing times often spills out as aggression in our politics. People cling to partisan parties that offer them a moral story—and those parties, in turn, seem to despise each other. In America, this hostility shows up in the conservative-versus-progressive divide. Of course, not everyone fits neatly into one camp or the other, but the framework still captures the tension that grips much of the nation.[8]

The two parties respond to rapid change in starkly different ways. For those who want to conserve a certain vision of American life, these are shaky times. When your priority is protecting a way of life, a way of thinking, or even a way of seeing reality, the breakneck pace of change feels like dangerous ground. With that instinct, slowing—or even stopping—change can feel like a moral duty. From this vantage point, agents of change aren't just opponents; they're threats. They're not ushering in a brighter future but dragging society toward a dystopian collapse. For those of us with more progressive inclinations, it is easy to conflate change with progress. These rapid changes can be perceived as the paving of the road to paradise. In the progressive worldview, preventing or slowing down change (particularly where justice is concerned) is viewed as oppressive and discriminatory. For progressives, the moral obligation flips. Instead of slowing change, they feel compelled to accelerate it—and to challenge anyone who tries to stand in the way. Now, obviously I am speaking in broad generalizations.

An increasing number of people do not neatly identify with either of the partisan clubs I have laid out for you. But I bring all this up to draw attention to an observation some thinkers have been warning about for years: This accelerated pace of change is coinciding with the rapid increase of political polarization and unparalleled distrust in each other and our institutions.

When I was a kid way back in the 1900s, political polarization was certainly a problem, but not to the extent it is today. There seemed to be a common understanding that how one voted once every four years was not sufficient rationale to break relationship with family, neighbors, friends, church members, or coworkers. We assumed that we all basically wanted the same thing, a free and prosperous society; we just had different ways of getting there.

Long gone are the days of assuming the best in our ideological opponents. Today for Christians and non-Christians alike, it is all too common to view those from the other party as dangerous. They're not just wrong, or stupid, or ignorant—they're evil. And we respond quite differently to evil people than we do to wrongheaded people. A person who's wrong can be tolerated, understood, enlightened, and even communed with. But an evil person? An evil person can only be stopped.

As social scientist and author Jonathan Haidt puts it, "Liberals and conservatives are opponents in the most literal sense, using the myth of pure evil to demonize the other side and unite their own."[9]

Our rapidly changing world has reshaped American politics—and not for the better. Hostility, suspicion, and disdain now run deep and at times even erupt into violence. Among Christians, this fear often shows itself in harsh, defensive responses, especially when conversations turn to politicized LGBTQ+ issues. The vitriol reveals just how much polarization has discipled our hearts.

A SPIRITUAL SHIFT

This rapid political shift came on the heels of a much more substantial spiritual shift. Spirituality in America is one of the fastest-changing sectors in our country. Sociologist Philip Rieff says the West is now a post-Christian culture.[10] According to Rieff, you can look at the history of Western spirituality in three eras. First, there was the pre-Christian culture, which lasted until roughly 300 BCE. In this era paganism, animal and human sacrifices, cultic practices, and idolatry (literal statues and images of divine beings) were mainstream. As the gospel spread and came to the West, and as imperialism worked its way into full steam, more pagan people adopted a Christian identity (some out of genuine conversion, some out of coercion).

This gave rise to a new era—a *Christian culture*—stretching from the fourth century to roughly the 1950s. During this time, the default worldview of the West was more or less Christian. But "Christianized" might be a more honest term. A culture itself cannot become Christian, but it can absorb Christian values, customs, and assumptions. In a Christianized society, you could count on your neighbors to share a basic belief in a Creator God, some knowledge of Jesus, and familiar categories like salvation, heaven and hell, religious holidays, and what it means to be "good." But it's crucial to distinguish between a Christianized culture and the actual call of Christ on his church—or between a

Christianized culture and the kingdom of heaven. These have too often been blurred together. Christianization never guaranteed faithful discipleship. The West's legacy of slavery, segregation, forceful conquest, racism, the subjugation of women, and yes, homophobia, bears witness to that. There is nothing Christian about these sins. Christianization simply meant that the cultural imagination was shaped by the schema of a Creator God and a redeeming Savior—even if the way of Jesus was lived far from faithfully. In the 1700s a little thing called the Enlightenment burst onto the scene. Also called the age of reason, this movement introduced a new era that prioritized naturalism, rationalism, and materialism above and beyond the spiritual. By the 1950s, as the Enlightenment gained steam and credibility in the marketplace of ideas, spirituality steadily became privatized.

There's a lot to thank the Enlightenment for—flushing toilets, air conditioning, smartphones stuffed with songs. The modern world would be unrecognizable without it—for better *and* for worse. The trouble began when Enlightenment thinkers and religious fundamentalists turned science and faith into enemies. It was a war no one needed, and everyone lost. Christians were branded as anti-science and anti-fact; scientists as anti-faith and atheistic. That false dichotomy sowed the seeds of today's culture wars, now woven into the fabric of American Christianity.[11]

In the wake of this shift, the world moved from *enchanted* to *disenchanted*—from seeing through a window into the divine to staring at the mirror of materialism. Philosopher Charles Taylor calls this mindset "the immanent frame": a world sealed off from transcendence, where nothing breaks in from beyond.[12] Theologian James K. A. Smith puts it bluntly: "When your ultimate conviction is that there is no eternal, you're most prone to absolutize the temporal."[13] That's the air we breathe now—a post-Christian culture where the sacred feels distant, the supernatural suspect, and the soul strangely flat.

Only a few decades ago, as early as the 1990s, more then 90 percent of Americans identified as Christian. Today that number is estimated to be around 64 percent. As of 2020, even before pandemic lockdown orders were put into effect, we reached a strange milestone in our country's history: It was the first time more than half of the country reported that they were not a part of any church. In the last twenty years, more people have left the church than came to church during the First Great Awakening, the Second Great Awakening, and Billy Graham's Crusades combined.[14]

America is the least churched it has ever been right now. And the religious "nones" are steadily increasing, most notably among millennials, Gen Z, and the Alpha generation.[15] These nones, so described because they select "none" in surveys asking about their religious affiliation, may be agnostic, atheist, or "spiritual but not religious." The nones are the fastest-growing demographic of spirituality in America, currently resting at about 30 percent and counting of the country's population.[16] We are a disenchanted people living in a disenchanted world. And Western culture no longer has the appearance of being "Christianized."

SHIFTING POWER DYNAMICS

Over the last three hundred years the Christian worldview has slowly but surely been decentered from popular society and a secular worldview has taken center stage. When we view this shift through the lens of Christ and his cause, we might be surprised and disappointed to see today's Christians engaging in culture wars, eager to make enemies of people who don't share their perspective. When we view it through the lens of power dynamics, Christians' eagerness to fight makes total sense.

Power is one hell of a drug. It is the most hotly contested resource in the world. And when people feel it slipping from their grasp, they often lash out. This is part of why many Christians are known for hostility toward LGBTQ+ people. They see rainbow flags in their neighborhoods, beloved characters on their screens, statistics warning of the nuclear family's decline—and they fear their faith is losing ground. To them, every step forward for the LGBTQ+ community feels like a step backward for Christianity. So they fight, desperate to reclaim the influence of another age.

But in chasing that power, Christians have done things that look nothing like Christ—spewing slurs, stoking fear, stirring violence, silencing dissent, clutching at control instead of bending to serve. In the scramble for dominance, loyalty to Jesus is often the first thing thrown aside.

And the cost? Our witness lies in ruins. LGBTQ+ neighbors, who should have been loved as image bearers for whom Christ bled, are cast as enemies in a political war. Fear reduces people to talking points. Love is replaced with suspicion. And when we bow to fear instead of Christ, we no longer live like him. We forget that the God who holds every era still holds this one.

REFLECTION QUESTIONS

1. How can focusing too much on one cultural issue cause us to miss or neglect other important kingdom concerns?

2. In what ways might culture wars foster hypocrisy within the church? How can we guard against this?
3. How does Jesus' call to take on his yoke (Matthew 11:29) challenge the mindset of cultural domination and conflict?

5

MORAL PANIC

Unaware that our culture has subverted our faith,
we lose a place from which to judge our own culture.

Miroslav Volf

The post went up sometime in the late afternoon:

> I'm DONE pretending this is normal. I will NOT let the satanic LGBTQ+ agenda confuse my child. Boys are boys and girls are girls. Marriage is between a man and a woman, and changing it to anything else is evil—end of story. What next, pedophilia is okay? Bestiality is just a sexual preference? This is war, and if you're not fighting, you're complicit. We have GOT to take our country back. The libs have too much power. I don't care who gets offended. I'm protecting my family. Feel free to unfollow me if you disagree. Say what you want, but at least Trump's not afraid to stand up to the LGBTQ+ insanity that's targeting our kids. It's about time someone with a spine fights for real families.

> I will not let this godless agenda confuse my child. We're taking America back for God—and I'm not sorry for saying it. #GodOverWoke #AmericaFirst #ProtectOurKids

Lori had been doomscrolling for hours that day—clicking through articles, comment threads, and outrage-laced videos about queer Pride being celebrated in schools. Her algorithm had been feeding her anxiety all day. Videos of children performing sexualized dances at drag shows, men and women sharing horror stories of their transition and detransition experiences, and more. Her anxiety was as high as ever. It wasn't the first time she'd posted something like this. But this one landed differently. It was sharper. Angrier. And it devastated someone she loved.

Unbeknownst to Lori, her son Eli saw the post. He had been wrestling with whether to come out to his mother. Not to provoke her. Not to make a statement. Just to be known.

He'd told me this a few nights earlier. Eli and I, along with another youth leader, were sitting in my office after youth group. "I've tried to imagine telling her," Eli said, staring at the floor. "But every time I hear her talk about gay people, it's like—she's talking about someone she hates. And I'm not sure what she'd do if she knew this about me."

He wasn't angry. Just tired. Worn down by the pressure of carrying a secret and the fear that the truth might cost him his mother's love. I wanted to believe it was all a misunderstanding—that surely Lori wouldn't reject her own son. But then I saw the post.

That's when it hit me: Lori didn't think she was attacking someone. She thought she was defending something. Her country.

Her family. Her faith. Her kid. And in her effort to protect Eli from the world, she had become the thing he feared most.

Many culture warriors feel justified by their impulse to fight for power, not purely because they are addressing weighty issues but because they don't see an incongruence between culture-warring and the way of Jesus. The ends seem to justify the means. But many of these American Christians have a misplaced sense of identity, and at the same time they're caught in a vicious cycle of anxiety.

Imagine a person trying to calm a storm by throwing rocks into the sea. The anxiety of watching the waves swell leads them to act, but their actions only stir the water more. In a similar way, many Christians, anxious over their perceived loss of cultural influence, throw themselves into "fighting the good fight" without pausing to consider whether the fight itself has been co-opted by a different spirit.

The identity crisis runs deep. Many have fused their Christian faith with the beliefs of their political tribe, such that defending one feels like defending the other. Much of American Christian witness today reflects an anxious energy: reactive, combative, and driven more by fear of cultural erosion than by hope in the resurrection. Until underlying anxiety and identity confusion are addressed, culture-warring will feel not only justified but virtuous.

MISPLACED IDENTITIES

When I was growing up, I did not think anyone could be a Democrat and a Christian at the same time. Those were diametrically opposed identities in my eyes. As a fiery conservative young adult, I felt more in common with my agnostic libertarian friends than

I did with my Christian Democrat friends. This should not have been so. It's not that my political identity was too entangled with my spiritual identity; it's that my political idolatry co-opted my allegiance to Jesus.

Politics have become one of the great shapers of our souls. They don't just influence our votes; they sculpt our identities, our choices, and our hopes. I don't care which party you back, but I care deeply where you anchor your identity. Because no matter what we say about "separation of church and state," there is no wall that can keep your politics from touching your discipleship. God will not be tricked by the compartments we build. And when we root our identity in the wrong soil, politics don't just divide us—they deform us, pulling Christ's followers into words and actions that bear little resemblance to Christ himself. Our identities become misplaced when we view our faith through the lens of our politics rather than our politics through the lens of our faith. Many evangelicals' relationship to politics is a perfect example of what Augustine calls "disordered loves": "When the miser prefers his gold to justice," he writes in his masterpiece *City of God*, "it is through no fault of the gold, but of the man. The fault does not lie in the thing loved, rather the disorder of his love."[1]

Our love for God should be the supreme affection of our hearts and the guiding force of our lives. Yet too often our loyalty to political tribes and candidates outpaces our devotion to him. Politics themselves are not sinful, but when they take priority over loving God by loving our neighbor—or when we stop letting faith be our compass in the political sphere—we step onto dangerous ground. If the church weren't so entangled with American politics—if we weren't clawing to preserve our power in a changing culture—our LGBTQ+ neighbors might see something beautiful in us instead of something to fear. But our political posturing has done real damage. It's made the church feel more like a threat than a refuge, more like a battlefield than a home. Instead of being a living sign that Christ is making all things new, we've too often been the noise drowning out his invitation. If our political identity gets in the way of following Jesus, then it's time to rethink who we are. Our identity in Christ isn't just one label among many; it's the foundation that gives shape and meaning to everything else. Calling ourselves conservative or progressive might offer some helpful insight into our perspectives, but those labels must remain secondary, tertiary, or lower. They can never take the lead over our primary calling as disciples of Jesus. Once we assume a Christian identity, it cannot be compartmentalized or separated from another identity marker that appeals to us.

In his book *Exiles: The Church in the Shadow of Empire*, Preston Sprinkle explains why the early church was viewed as such a threat to the Roman Empire. As recounted in Acts 19, Paul's gospel proclamation to the citizens of Ephesus sent the city into an uproar. Why did the gospel outrage the Ephesians to such a degree? These Roman thinkers we not intimidated by another God joining the conversation. After all, they had tolerated Jewish monotheism for centuries.

The sticking point was this notion that Jesus was Lord. You see, the expression "Jesus is Lord" was politically subversive in that context. Roman citizens already had someone they were required to call "Lord," and his name was Caesar. In the Roman world you could have many gods, but you could have only one Lord. If Jesus was Lord, then Caesar was not. The chaos in Ephesus was not merely a spiritual issue but a political one. Sprinkle writes:

> This is where our watered-down, de-politicized understanding of church can mislead us. It fogs up our interpretive lenses and prevents us from appreciating the true scandal of Paul's message. Paul didn't throw Ephesus into an uproar by doing "churchy" things, like preaching sermons about a private savior who touched hearts without touching politics. Rather, Paul proclaimed that Jesus is Lord, and this was a politically disruptive thing to say.[2]

The implications of this account are startling. In the ancient world there was no separating your political identity from your spiritual self. And I would contend the same is true today, try as we might to compartmentalize. However, Christian nationalism and political idolatry distort this relationship in a way that privileges politics over faith. It takes the radical call to love God and love neighbor and reduces it to the crude and thoroughly unbiblical "God and country." As Esau McCaulley writes, "Christian nationalism has always sought to baptize the sinful parts of American history. It wants to hide our sin, not confess it."[3]

Ancient Israel was repeatedly rebuked in the Old Testament for their worship of idols in the "high places." Today, the idols we worship and our "high places" can be found on Capitol Hill. To have a political identity that in any way runs against the grain of following Jesus is to have an idol. I am not trying to sway your political leanings. I would just caution us, in the words of my friend Joshua Ryan Butler, to "not let your lean become a kneel."[4]

Likewise, Dr. A. J. Swoboda warns that we tend to look to politics for what can be found only in God. This puts us on a dangerous road. He writes, "In lieu of worshipping God, politics has become our new religion, policy its theology, and social media posts the new great commission. But can politics replace God's face as the sustaining force of society?"[5]

Politics cannot give us what only God can give us. When a political identity is at the center of our being and our political tribe tells us who we are, we see success only in terms of power gained. And when our power is threatened, we will wage war. On the other hand, a Christian identity sees success only in the will of God. Dietrich Bonhoeffer beautifully contends that the entirety of the Christian life can be boiled down to one thing: to seek the will of God and align ourselves with it.[6] And how do we recognize the will of God? If it looks, sounds, tastes, smells, or feels like Jesus, we're probably on the right track.

A sure sign our political identity bows to our Christian identity is when we can name the ways our tribes clash with the Gospels. Because when I read the Gospels, I can't find Jesus marching in lockstep with Republicans or Democrats. If we fit too comfortably in either camp, we are probably out of step with the kingdom of God. What I need, what you need, what our LGBTQ+ neighbors need is not another party anxiously clamoring for power. We need the living presence of the kingdom breaking in here and now, demanding our allegiance and offering us life.

A VICIOUS CYCLE OF ANXIETY

Another reason Christians choose culture-warring, even when it is harmful to Christ's cause, is that we are caught up in a self-perpetuating cycle of anxiety. Given how loaded with anxiety and outrage the conversation surrounding LGBTQ+ people and the church can be, we can't overstate the importance of understanding this cycle.

Anxiety is widespread, contagious, and often so commonplace that we can't even detect it. Anxiety is the air we breathe and the water we swim in. Our air and our water are poisoned by a difficult-to-detect, almost ambient level of terror originating from the belief that humanity and civilization are at the pinnacle of progress.

Edwin Friedman was a famed family therapist who popularized the work surrounding family systems theory and differentiated leadership originally pioneered by Murray Bowen. Friedman's work stemmed from his time shepherding people as a rabbi in his local synagogue. His work spread throughout other synagogues, then churches, and eventually world-renowned leadership spaces. Friedman argues that, contrary to popular belief, we are not holistically progressing as a species. Yes, scientific and humanitarian efforts are indeed progressing. But emotionally and relationally, we are regressing. Friedman writes:

> The climate of contemporary America has become so chronically anxious that our society has gone into an emotional regression that is toxic. . . . It has lowered people's pain thresholds, with the result that comfort is valued over the rewards of facing challenge, symptoms come in fads, and cures go in and out of style like clothing fashions. . . . The anxiety is so deep within the emotional processes of our nation that it is almost as though a neurosis has become nationalized.[7]

As a culture we have never had more than we have right now. We've never had more money, equality, educational opportunity, resources for mental and physical health, or technological advancement than we do at this moment in time. And we have never been more isolated or anxious. Former Nebraska Senator Ben Sasse writes, "In the midst of extraordinary prosperity we are also living through a crisis. Our communities are collapsing and people are feeling more isolated, adrift, and purposeless than ever."[8]

Our belief that we should be progressing while in significant ways we are regressing creates what Friedman calls a cycle of anxiety. This cycle can exist within any network of relationships. It can exist in families, churches, friend groups, workplaces, political parties, and entire nations. As long as people live anxiously, this cycle feeds itself and perpetuates itself.

The history of Christians' relationship to our LGBTQ+ neighbors consists of a series of anxiety-fueled culture wars. And this anxious-cycle framework helps us understand why we are so prone to take up arms. Understanding it can help us manage and defuse our anxiety, enabling us to extend non-anxious love to our LGBTQ+ neighbors.

According to Friedman, there are five characteristics to this cycle of anxiety. Let's look at each in turn.

Reactivity. Reactivity is "a vicious cycle of intense reactions of each member to events and to one another."[9] This is the emotional domino effect—each person's outrage triggering another's until everyone's trembling. It's what happens when we see a headline, a post, or a clip that lights up our nervous system like a siren. The cause may feel noble, the outrage justified. But so often, our passion is just anxiety wearing a moral costume.

Take drag queens reading children's books in libraries. Drag queen story hour was a program that started in San Francisco in 2015 but didn't gain steam as a culture-war issue until the end of the 2010s. This program ignited anxiety on one side of the political aisle, with conservatives worrying it would lead to the sexualization or grooming of children. Progressives became anxious in response, dismissing the other side's concerns as the musings of transphobes and homophobes. Both sides responded in highly anxious, highly reactive ways.[10]

The ideas that cause reactivity within people groups are usually the ideas the groups perceive as moral violations. Thus, anxiety-fueled reactivity is framed as a moral battle. This reactivity then instigates the next phase in the cycle of anxiety.

Herding. Herding is defined as "a process through which the forces for togetherness triumph over the forces for individuality and move everyone to adapt to the least mature members."[11] Our collective anxiety drives us into herds. We gather, fueled less by vision than by outrage. And in these groups, we rarely rise to strength—we sink to the level of the least mature among us. The loudest fear, the sharpest outrage sets the tone. In a reactive crowd, power belongs not to the wise but to the most anxious, and the whole group bends to their trembling energy.

When we do this, we take on the sociological quality of tribalism. Anxiety and outrage unite us against a common enemy, and this makes us tribal. That is, we are suspicious of or directly opposed to anyone who isn't "us." This propagates the "us vs. them" mentality that seems to define our cultural moment.

Tribalism can have dangerous ramifications. These tribal instincts bind and blind us, and they can make us complicit in unspeakable horrors. We need only to look at Nazi Germany, lynchings in the segregated South, and chairman Mao's genocide to see this is true. All of those atrocities were perpetrated by groups of people bound and blinded by a herding instinct.

We see this herding instinct throughout the LGBTQ+ conversation. Both sides of the polarized arena of LGBTQ+ issues rally each other around the idea that the other side is the adversarial, nefarious opponent that must be stopped. When this herding characteristic is in effect, we arrive at the next characteristic of the cycle.

Blame displacement. Blame displacement is "an emotional state in which family members focus on forces that have victimized them rather than taking responsibility for their own being and destiny."[12] Reactivity and tribalism always lead us to make enemies of another person, group, or tribe. When this happens, rather taking inventory of our lives and self-evaluating, we are quick to throw blame at the "other." This lets us avoid taking responsibility.

Blame displacement suffocates growth and prevents renewal. It resists self-examination and keeps us trapped in our shortcomings, sin, and bad habits. These are things we overcome through union with God and with others and through personal ownership over our lives. When we blame some other group for our plight, we never grow and we never heal.

In the church's culture war with LGBTQ+ people, we have seen the church assign a lot of blame. LGBTQ+ people have been blamed for the loss of family values in America, moral decay, and more. Some public Christian commentators have even blamed LGBTQ+ people for disastrous events like 9/11 and Hurricane Katrina, with claims that their moral depravity wrought God's judgment on our nation.

When divorce rates for heterosexual marriages are just as high inside the church as on the outside, we have some blame to take for the loss of family values. For much of human history, heterosexual men have been given the green light (or at the very least a yellow light) to exert sexual dominance over nonconsenting victims. They've been given passes and had excuses made for them, and they've been told "boys will be boys." I doubt we can honestly blame LGBTQ+ people for widespread cultural perversion in light of this. Blame displacement is alive and well in this conversation.

Quick fix mentality. Blame displacement leads to the next phase of the anxious cycle: a quick fix mentality. This is "a low threshold for pain that constantly seeks symptom relief rather than fundamental change."[13]

When we have a quick fix mentality, we oversimplify nuanced situations, vilify complicated people, and consistently give in to instant gratification. Instant gratification gives us a low tolerance for discomfort and an inability to cope with unpleasant feelings. A quick fix mentality prioritizes what we want now over what we desire most, which, for most of us, is true, deep, inner healing.

This quick fix mentality has prevented many well-meaning Christians and church leaders from speaking meaningfully to their LGBTQ+ neighbors. I experienced this personally in my journey. After I came forward and shared my story publicly, plenty of friends and family members were eager to offer a quick fix.

"You must have been fooled by one of Satan's lies. If you disbelieve the lie, God won't leave you in your sexual brokenness."

"You must have had an overbearing mother and an unaffectionate father."

"God wants full redemption for you. If you pray more and confess your sins, he'll free you from your same-sex attractions."

"If you want all God has for you, you won't accept your same-sex attraction. You'll fight it."

I heard all of these and more from Christians caught up in the cycle of anxiety, leaving them grasping at quick fixes. These crude oversimplifications belittle the deeply complex forces that make a person who they are. They assume God's plan is for everyone to be a heterosexual. They lack the nuance needed to foster intimacy with a person.

A quick fix mentality keeps us from addressing core problems. And all of this is fueled by the fifth characteristic in this cycle.

Lack of differentiated leadership. Lack of differentiated leadership is defined as "a failure of nerve that stems from and contributes to the first four" steps in the cycle of anxiety.[14]

This cycle is perpetuated by emotionally bankrupt leaders, and it creates more emotionally bankrupt leaders. These leaders cannot differentiate themselves from the group, and they are capable only of spreading anxiety, not defusing it. Compare how presidential hopefuls talk to one another nowadays to how they interacted in decades past. Past candidates seemed less likely to pour kerosene on the fire of our fears than those in action today.

In his 2008 bid for president, John McCain defended his political opponent's character at the Republican Nation Convention. When a member of the crowd brought up an unfounded conspiracy theory about Barack Obama, McCain responded, "He is a decent man, a family man that I just happen to have disagreements with on fundamental issues."[15] A moment like this at either the Republican National Convention or the Democratic National Convention seems like a fairy tale these days. Our national leaders are anxious people, contending to lead an anxious nation, fueled by an anxious cycle.

Pastors, church leaders, and family leaders can easily fall into this lack of differentiation. This plays out in at least four significant ways.

1. Failure of nerve. An undifferentiated pastor might make decisions based on fear of conflict or desire for approval rather than deep biblical reflection. For instance, they might suddenly affirm or condemn LGBTQ+ relationships in response to congregational pressure, media trends, or emotional conversations without a consistent or scripturally grounded position. Pastors can lose the nerve required to clearly lead and teach in alignment with their convictions.

One pastor I know will not touch the topic of sexuality or gender identity from the pulpit with a ten-foot pole. He believes it will only frustrate people and fears the backlash theological clarity might bring him. Another pastor I know refuses to speak publicly about the ways the church has failed LGBTQ+ people, believing the people of his church will call him "affirming" or "woke" and leave. Thus members of his church are permitted to worship with hard hearts unchecked.

In the Bible, we see Peter experience this failure of nerve. In John 18:15-18 and 25-27 we see Peter's infamous denial of knowing Christ. As Jesus is being interrogated and wrongly accused by the

Jewish high counsel, Peter watches from a distance. Eventually, people start to recognize Peter as one of Jesus' followers. The tides are shifting on people's opinion of Jesus. It is no longer advantageous or safe to be associated with him.

Just as Jesus predicted at their final meal together, Peter denies Christ three times before the rooster crows. In his anxiety, Peter overidentifies with the anxiety of the mob and underidentifies with his truest convictions. His act of denial is textbook failure of nerve.

2. *Failure of heart.* The flip side of a failure of nerve is a failure of heart. If a failure of nerve surrenders conviction to keep the crowd happy, a failure of heart sacrifices compassion on the altar of being right. A pastor, parent, or friend experiences a failure of heart when they use theology to contradict a biblical vision of human value and the *imago Dei*.

We see Christian communities experience failure of heart toward LGBTQ+ people all the time. We see it in the ways we have chosen judgment over grace, fear over love, and prejudice over curiosity. To avoid moral or theological compromise, many Christians suffer from a failure of heart. The tragedy is, in Christ's economy of mercy, a failure of heart *is* moral and theological compromise.

In Luke 22:1-6 Judas agrees to betray Jesus for a measly thirty pieces of silver. Jesus more than likely has proved a disappointment to Judas. His teachings and practice of enemy love and extravagant generosity stand in stark contrast with Judas's desire for a bloodthirsty and wealthy Messiah. In this disappointment, Judas becomes disconnected from his love for Jesus and overconnected with his myopic moral vision. All of this leads to a devastating failure of heart for Judas.

3. Emotional enmeshment. An undifferentiated leader, parent, or friend might feel personally responsible for how others *feel* about their stance. For example, if someone is hurt by the church's position on sexuality, the pastor might take on that pain in a way that leads to guilt-driven leadership or emotionally manipulative decision-making. A parent may cave on their deeper convictions when one of their children comes out to them; they may find themself unable to honor the courage of their convictions for fear of conflict or being rejected by their child.

Rather than staying rooted in conviction while remaining relationally connected to all parties, the leader or parent might lean too heavily on doctrinal propositions, cut off dialogue with others, demonize dissent, or make theological issues personal and tribal.

4. Loss of spiritual wisdom. Because of this internal anxiety and external pressure, the leader or parent may no longer function as a peacemaking presence—someone who is emotionally steady, relationally present, and theologically grounded. Instead, they may mirror the anxiety of the system they find themselves in and cease to be a source of calm or direction.

Pastor and leadership consultant Steve Cuss has been sounding the alarm for years: Anxiety is contagious. You can catch it like a cold.[16] If this is true, then for too many years too many Christians have been superspreaders of this anxious cycle. We have looked more like followers of the prince of fear than the Prince of peace.

DAMAGED WITNESS

This culture-war mindset has severely damaged the church's witness to LGBTQ+ people. When the church leads with outrage and anxiety instead of compassion, it communicates that LGBTQ+ individuals are problems to solve rather than people to love. Our posture matters when we are holding to historic convictions. Jesus calls his followers to be peacemakers, not power brokers (Matthew 5:9). If our message is delivered through fear and political aggression, we distort the gospel and drive people further from the one who welcomed the marginalized with both truth and tenderness. Scripture teaches us to "be merciful, just as your Father is merciful" (Luke 6:36). We are to be tenderhearted people reflecting our merciful God.

ELI AND LORI

Eli was a senior in high school when he came out to me after youth group. Having stumbled across side B Christianity on social media, he was resolute in his devotion to the historic Christian sexual ethic.[17] But he knew he couldn't hide anymore, and he asked me to sit with him when he told his parents.

I mediated the conversation, and the fear and pain on Lori's face was unmistakable. Tears filled her eyes. Knowing my story, Lori asked me what I thought of all of this.

"Lori, this is such a heavy, complicated thing," I said. "But what matters most is that you raised a kid who loves the Lord. And that, even though he experiences something that many leave the faith over, he is choosing to stick with it, and honor God in it all. I think that's special."

Lori nodded her head in agreement, face still heavy with grief. Over the next year I would mediate many more conversations between Eli and Lori. I urged Lori to lay off the clickbait news articles, talking heads behind news desks, and social media outrage.

I encouraged her to pray more, read more Scripture, and muster the inner fortitude to be more motivated by love than fear.

It has been several years since I have talked with Lori or Eli. But I keep tabs on them on social media from time to time. Lori has stopped posting anxiety-filled paragraphs, and Eli went to seminary. Every once in a while one of them will post a photo of their family together. No sorrow or grief to be found.

REFLECTION QUESTIONS

1. How does Friedman's cycle of anxiety show up in conversations about LGBTQ+ issues within the church?
2. In what ways can anxiety-driven reactions harm the church's ability to witness to Christ's love and truth?
3. What are some signs that a family, church, or leader is caught in the cycle of anxiety?

6

UNGODLY THEOLOGY

Biblical orthodoxy without compassion is surely the ugliest thing in the world.

Francis Schaeffer

Luke 18:35-43 is one of my favorite stories in the whole Bible. In it we see Jesus, his disciples, and a parade of followers walking down Jericho Road. By this point Jesus has attracted much attention through his miracles, teachings, and general fragrance of heaven. As he travels, the passage tells us, a crowd follows him (Luke 18:36).

On this road they come upon a blind beggar. Houseless. Dirty. Disabled. In the ancient world, as is still true today, there was no one more marginalized, at risk, or shunned than a disabled transient person. This blind beggar was also associated with religious shame. In a parallel passage in the Gospel of John, Jesus' disciples ask, "Who sinned, this man or his parents, that he was born blind?" (John 9:2). This question reveals how society perceived the man and more than likely how he perceived himself.

It wasn't uncommon in ancient times to see physical infirmity as a punishment from God. A harmful and misguided view to be sure, but one that was fairly common. So when Jesus' followers saw the blind beggar in Luke 18, empathy and compassion were not their first response. They more likely would have judged him, condemned him, and made assumptions about his or his parents' misdeeds. They may have felt disdain. There was no place for a blind beggar in their world.

And yet apparently this blind man had heard stories about the miracle-performing rabbi. Jesus was often homeless himself. Maybe this beggar knew that and thought Jesus would sympathize with him. So the beggar does a bold thing for a man of his social status. He cries out, "Jesus, Son of David, have mercy on me!" (Luke 18:38).

The way this man addresses Jesus is telling. He calls him "Son of David." He shouts his belief that Jesus is the Messiah, emerging from the line of David, destined to restore Israel. This confession is not something many of Jesus' contemporaries are willing to make. And notice the request. He doesn't say, "Jesus, heal me!" He doesn't ask for sight or for wealth to get out of his station in life. He has gone without many things his whole life, but there is one thing he wants Jesus to provide more than anything else. Mercy. This blind beggar asks Jesus to notice him and care about him.

It's a well-known reality that the more we have, the more we want. Human beings' sense of longing will always be stronger than our sense of satisfaction. But when we don't have anything, when we've spent our whole life cast aside, dirty, and left out, what we want more than anything is to know we are noticed and cared for. What we want is mercy.

Of course, it's in Jesus' wheelhouse to stop and listen to this man's cry. You'd think that by this point it would be intuitive for the disciples as well. But that's not what happens. In verse 39 we read, "Those who led the way rebuked him." It was probably the twelve disciples leading the way. Likely Peter, James, and John, Jesus' inner circle leadership team.

These men rebuked the beggar and tried to put him in his place. They might have said something like, "This is the Messiah. The hope of Israel rests on his shoulders. The King of the world. You are judged by God. A blind beggar. This Messiah isn't for you. How dare you even speak to him?"

Here is someone literally crying out for a touch from Jesus. He fits the exact profile of the types of disgraced people Jesus stopped to heal countless times up to this point. But Jesus' students, his representatives, rebuke him. Standing between a man crying out for Jesus and Jesus himself are the disciples.

This is an all-too-familiar picture.

What the disciples don't realize is that this blind beggar isn't going to comply with their rebuke. He's probably an Eight on the Enneagram, because the next thing the text tells us is, "He shouted all the more, 'Son of David, have mercy on me!'" (Luke 18:39). This is incredibly brave. It would not have been socially acceptable for this blind beggar to let out a defiant cry after the disciples' rebuke.

What is the result? Jesus does exactly what you'd expect him to do. He heals the blind man. The blind man praises God. The crowds of people offer praise to God in response to Jesus' power and mercy.

In this story, a plethora of barriers stood between the blind man and Jesus. All of them were rooted in ungodly theology. Ungodly theological barriers also stand between all types of people—particularly LGBTQ+ people—and the church today. I am willing to bet there has rarely been a LGBTQ+ person in church who has not felt, on some level, like this blind beggar. Growing up terrified and in the closet, wanting desperately to love and follow Jesus, I rarely had the courage to raise my voice above the many rebuking voices around me. But Jesus models a path beyond the rebuke. Understanding these barriers empowers us to move beyond them and imitate Jesus.

A MALFORMED THEOLOGY OF GOD

How we see God determines how we see everything else. As A. W. Tozer famously wrote:

> What comes into our minds when we think about God is the most important thing about us. The history of mankind will probably show that no people has ever risen above its religion, and man's spiritual history will positively demonstrate that no religion has ever been greater than its idea of God. . . . We tend by a secret law of the soul to move toward our mental image of God. This is true not only of the individual Christian, but of the company of Christians that composes the Church. Always the most revealing thing about the Church is her idea of God.[1]

If as believers we "move toward our mental image of God," then one of the most important tasks a Christian faces is to behold

God clearly and accurately. Luckily, we don't have to look further than Jesus to see a perfected revelation of God (see John 14:19, Hebrews 1:3, and 1 Timothy 3:16, among many others). Ungodly theology can be traced to a lack of attention to Christ. If Jesus is the focal point of our theology (theology being the study of God), then our lives will reveal him. But Christlike theology has been woefully absent in our understanding of our LGBTQ+ neighbors. Well-intended attempts at doctrinal purity have frequently forgone the love of Christ, and when the love of Christ is absent, our doctrine will always be ungodly.

Doctrine, no matter how many Bible verses are attached to it or how thoroughly it has been theologically systematized, is never an end in itself. It is meant to serve love, to lead us into deeper communion with God and neighbor. As Paul writes, "The goal of this command is love, which comes from a pure heart and a good conscience and a sincere faith" (1 Timothy 1:5). When doctrine becomes a weapon to exclude, control, or elevate oneself above others, it ceases to reflect the heart of the One who is truth incarnate. Jesus did not say the world would know us by our doctrinal accuracy, but by our love (John 13:35). Without love, doctrine becomes a lifeless idol—orthodoxy turned in on itself, divorced from the Spirit who gives life. As Paul famously warns, "If I have the gift of prophecy and can fathom all mysteries and all knowledge . . . but do not have love, I am nothing" (1 Corinthians 13:2).

A MALFORMED THEOLOGY OF FALLEN HUMANITY

Shortly after I came forward with my story of being same-sex-attracted, and after being released from my job as youth pastor, I had a disturbing interaction with the parent of one of my students. I was stopped after church and confronted about unfounded rumors regarding my "homosexual deviancy." He said, "Is it true that you're homosexual? Did you do anything to my kid? I trusted you with my son."

When I asked what he meant, praying he hadn't meant to insinuate what he clearly had, the parent went on to inform me that he believed same-sex attraction was a slippery slope to pedophilia (a pernicious and misleading theory with no data to support it). He explained to me that same-sex attraction was a chosen path of sin. He said God would not allow me to experience same-sex attraction unless I nurtured desires for it. He insisted that I, on some level, must have chosen it. And if I was willing to choose that form of "depraved evil" (his words, not mine), the Lord would give me even more depraved desires. In this case, pedophilia.

I assured him that my same-sex attraction had not led to a struggle with pedophilia. I also told him I found the notion that God would give people immoral desires, like pedophilia, deeply objectionable (not to mention a blatant misapplication of Romans 1:24).

This led to an awkward back-and-forth, where I repeatedly had to tell him my same-sex attraction would never lead me to touch, nor even want to touch, a child. I felt a little bit like Frankenstein's monster being chased by an angry mob with their torches and pitchforks, like I was a threat to the innocence and safety of the community.

I drove home from church that day sobbing the entire car ride. Eventually my wife and I stopped attending church for almost a year.

This interaction was ten years ago, and I have had the gift of time, hindsight, counseling, and more Christlike theology to sort through it. Why was this man so hesitant to believe me, whom he had known closely for most of my life, and so quick to believe I'd be capable of such a vile thing? Because my story—that my experience of same-sex attraction was unwanted, unchosen, and certainly not a slippery slope to pedophilia—did not confirm the theological story he believed. In other words, my story did not confirm his bias.

Confirmation bias is our built-in echo chamber. It's the tendency to notice only what agrees with our views and dismiss what doesn't. We cling to the evidence that props up our beliefs and quietly ignore the rest. This bias shapes how we read, watch, remember, and even pray—bending reality to fit our assumptions. It reinforces stereotypes, deepens polarization, and keeps us trapped in the illusion that we're always right.

Unfortunately, this man was far from the only person to tell me same-sex attraction was a pathway to pedophilia, bestiality, or other forms of sexual brokenness. Many evangelicals raised in the epoch of purity culture have been taught that abnormal forms of sexual immorality are a gateway to more horrifying forms of sexual depravity. This is due to a bad interpretation of Romans 1:24, which reads, "Therefore God gave them over in the sinful desires of their hearts to sexual impurity for the degrading of their bodies with one another."

The way this passage had been taught to me, and the way this man interpreted said passage, was that if you experience a sinful sexual desire of some kind and do not rid yourself of it, God will give you even more depraved sexual longings as an act of judgment.

The problem is, this passage isn't talking about the mere existence of a desire. And it isn't saying God will add more debased desires to your pervert résumé if you don't cleanse yourself of your existing immoral desires. This passage is about the excessive indulgence of lust, which is hardly the same thing as experiencing an attraction to something or someone. It is not saying God will compound your sexual immorality, as if God would debase himself to be complicit with sin. Understood in context, Romans 1:24 is saying that when our hearts are set on something other than God, God is not going to force you to stay with him.

Commenting on this passage, Karl Barth writes, "The wrath of God consists precisely in this: that man is permitted to go his own way. Man's separation from God, the movement of the creature away from the Creator, carries its own penalty with it."[2]

The man I spoke with did not know what to do with a same-sex-attracted person who did not choose or want those desires. To him, this meant God had somehow allowed me to experience same-sex attraction independent of my cooperation. That tension was too uncomfortable for him. It might require him to call into question the people responsible for his own theological formation. It might even force him to reconsider the way he talked about, thought about, and treated gay people.

My existence and my statements were a challenge to the story he already believed about God and about people like me. For him, it was easier to write me off than to reconsider his stories. If we're being honest, I think most of us can relate to this. Rather than seriously probe our theologies and stances, rather than testing them scrupulously, we take the path of least resistance. Even if it hurts another.

This conversation reinforced a narrative I'd held since I knew about my orientation: I was a monster and not safe to be with in community. Countless others in my shoes have had these same thoughts. When you go to church to worship, learn, and fellowship, and then you are accused of unspeakable things, it becomes difficult to attend church with any sense of safety, belonging, or joy.

The idea that same-sex attraction is a slippery slope to pedophilia is not only untrue (again, there is no data to support this correlation), it is also completely unfounded in Scripture. It is also untrue that God is unkind or unjust in allowing some people to experience same-sex attraction without their choosing. We all experience longings and desires we have to say "no" to. This is not an LGBTQ+ thing; it's a human thing. The notion that these struggles can simply be prayed away with faith and obedience is more rooted in the prosperity gospel than it is in Scripture or the historic witness of the church.

The more we can eliminate these untrue and unhelpful theological barriers, the more we are free to find the actual truth in Scripture. With this barrier removed, our LGBTQ+ neighbors can sit at our tables and in our church buildings with the ability to discover the beauty and power of a life set apart for the purposes of God. At the very least, they can come without being treated with suspicion and accusation. It's a low bar, but even that will be relief to some LGBTQ+ people.

A MALFORMED THEOLOGY OF FAMILY

Similar to how the beggar's blindness posed a barrier for him in the ancient world, same-sex attraction and gender dysphoria pose difficult barriers in our world. While many LGBTQ+ people would understandably object to the suggestion that their orientation is a condition akin to blindness, the parallel is appropriate.

Dr. Mark Yarhouse's "disability lens" helps us make sense of the LGBTQ+ experience in light of creation and fall. It sees same-sex attraction and gender dysphoria as nonmoral conditions—symptoms of a broken world and not deliberate sin. This perspective keeps us from both condemnation and celebration, grounding us instead in realism and grace. He writes, "From this perspective, same-sex attraction is understood to be a result of living in a fallen world. . . . The aim is not to condemn, but to respond with compassion and support."[3]

Like anyone else who experiences a disability in a world built for able-bodied people, LGBTQ+ people come into church with an innate sense that they're entering a world not made for them. To be a gay or trans person in a standard evangelical church is to be in a culture completely centered around marriage and, in some churches, very specific gender roles. It's not hard to imagine the problems this poses for a same-sex-attracted person called to singleness or a gender-dysphoric woman who would rather throw axes than go to a tea party.

Rather than reflecting the family of God revealed in the book of Acts, many evangelical churches are structured around the paradigm of the nuclear family and overly rigid gender expectations. And that culture functions well enough for folks who can fit the mold. But it is impossibly hard for people who do not or cannot fit.

The family of God in the New Testament included people from virtually every walk of life. Rich, poor, slave, free, Jew, Gentile, male, female, young, old, single, and married. The New Testament vision of God's family is that of a large tent with a huge table, with room for all our stories. This vision of family has led Christianity to become the most diverse global movement in human history. Contrast this with the vision of the nuclear family, more championed by American conservative customs than New Testament wisdom. In the nuclear family you have a mom and dad, some kids, and maybe a grandparent or two. This vision of family is too small for the church.

In *Households of Faith: Practicing Family in the Kingdom of God*, theologian Emily Hunter McGowin offers a compelling reimagining of what Christian families can and should be. Her explanation resists idolizing the nuclear household and instead roots family life in the self-giving love of God. Rather than beginning with the Genesis account of Adam and Eve to define family, McGowin begins with Jesus, who radically expanded the boundaries of familial belonging. He spoke of spiritual kinship that transcends blood ties, declaring that whoever does the will of the Father is his brother, sister, and mother. This Christ-centered starting point reframes the family not as a closed biological unit but as an open, Spirit-formed community of mutual care.

McGowin describes the family as an "apprenticeship to love," a space where people learn to give and receive grace in daily rhythms of vulnerability, forgiveness, and service.[4] This vision challenges churches that exalt a narrow model of family based on marriage and childrearing. Instead, McGowin calls for families in all their diversity to be places where love is practiced and perfected, with church communities extending the definition of family to include single people, celibate people, widows, the childless, the elderly, and those who have found chosen family amid rejection or loss.

This expansive vision has profound implications for how the church might welcome LGBTQ+ people. When churches treat the nuclear family as the gold standard of Christian life, they implicitly render anyone outside of it—especially queer believers—as spiritually incomplete. But if, as McGowin argues, the family of God is defined not by biology or conformity to a 1950s ideal but by shared participation in the life and love of Christ, then the church can become a place of real belonging. It can be the household where no one is left out, where love is not limited by category, and where every person is invited to both give and receive as a vital member of the body.

There is deep ache in being same-sex attracted or gender dysphoric. It's the fear of being cast out. The loneliness of celibacy. The quiet grief of not fitting anywhere—not in the world, not even in your own skin. For some, it's the revulsion toward their own bodies; for others, it's the longing to be seen without being shamed. Following Jesus as an LGBTQ+ person is no easy road, especially when the church often exalts the nuclear family as the pinnacle of holiness.

Part of the beauty of the New Testament church is that it finds a way for all types of people to fit in. Consider Jesus and the Samaritan woman at the well in John 4, Peter and the household of Cornelius in Acts 10, or Philip and the Ethiopian eunuch in Acts 8. Sexual orientation and gender dysphoria come with pain on their own. When the church models the beauty of inclusion and the ethos of our earliest fathers and mothers, it will alleviate that pain, not contribute to it.

A MALFORMED THEOLOGY OF DISCIPLESHIP

Then there is a malformed theology of discipleship. We see this in the way Jesus' disciples erected barriers for the blind beggar rather than paving the way to Jesus for him. Once the beggar mustered the courage to speak up and ask to be dignified, rather than serving him, loving him, and joyfully bringing him to the feet of Jesus, what did the disciples do? They rebuked him. They shut him down. They told him to be quiet and to know his place.

While that is sad, it's somewhat of a relief to know this phenomenon we're talking about, of Christians erecting barriers between Jesus and people who need him, isn't new. Western Christians are not the first followers of Jesus in church history to do this. The problem goes back to the first disciples. We are not uniquely flawed, corrupt, or innovative in our shortcomings. Because this phenomenon is so ancient, there are also many examples of how to correct it.

Here's where we get to better news. Our teacher, Jesus, shows us exactly how to respond. He breaks down manmade barriers to bring healing to the rejected.

The disciples likely thought they were doing Jesus a favor by rebuking this blind beggar. They thought this was what Jesus would have wanted. You see, the disciples believed that Jesus was preparing to raise up an army to destroy the Roman Empire and bring freedom to the nation of Israel. Jesus didn't have time for blind beggars, they likely assumed. He had an oppressive empire to destroy.

This scene offers a striking parallel to how many Christians treat LGBTQ+ individuals today. Like the crowd who saw the beggar as a disruption, churches often treat LGBTQ+ people the same way—discouraging them from sharing their stories, asking hard questions, or seeking spiritual support unless they conform to predetermined expectations. Instead of welcoming their honest cries for connection with God, Christians have often responded with discomfort, avoidance, or rebuke.

In much of the modern church, gatekeeping has taken too high a precedent in our discipleship journey. Our energy is often spent evaluating who's "in" or "out," who's ready or who's not, rather than inviting people into the lifelong process of walking with Jesus. We've mistaken our role, acting more like bouncers at the door of the kingdom than servants within it.

But the gospel never calls us to control access. It calls us to make disciples. That requires hospitality, not suspicion. Instead of gatekeepers of the kingdom, we must learn to take the posture of hosts at Christ's table—welcoming the wounded, the questioning, the messy, and the seeking. Discipleship begins with invitation, not interrogation. Jesus' ministry was marked by tables, not checkpoints. If we truly believe he is the one who transforms hearts, our job is not to screen for worthiness but to extend the invitation and walk alongside people as they discover what it means to follow him.

The church, intentionally or not, often becomes more like the crowd than the Christ we follow—dismissing, silencing, and distancing those who cry out. In doing so, it not only harms LGBTQ+ people but also misses the heart of the gospel, which is always moving toward the outcast, the overlooked, and the one calling out for mercy.

A MALFORMED THEOLOGY OF RESTORATION

"Tony, I don't like that you make light of your sexual brokenness," a fellow pastor once told me.

Caught off guard by his remark, I responded, "What do you mean?"

"You talk so casually about being same-sex-attracted. You even joke around with some of your friends about it. But this is not funny. This is a serious sin you need to take to the Lord, and I'd love to help you with it."

"Well, there's a difference between being affected by the fall and participating in sin," I explained. "My orientation is a defect of the fall, but my desires, when surrendered to Jesus, are not sinful. To be fallen is to experience the consequence of sin and chaos; to be sinful is to add to it. I do take this seriously. I'm faithful to my wife, I am careful in my relational boundaries, and I have studied this more than any other area of theology. I don't know how to take it more seriously."

"It just feels like you don't want all God has for you when you say that. I believe God wants to totally heal you and restore you from same-sex attraction. There are prayer ministries and therapeutic practices that have been proven to help people like you."

I thanked the earnest pastor and explained that I would not go down that road again. I've done the therapeutic practices, I've done the deliverance prayers, and all those things did was build my animosity toward God. This suggestion, well-meaning though it was, was rooted in a false belief about sexuality and Christian faithfulness.

In evangelical spaces, when discussing LGBTQ+ people we tend to equate righteousness with heterosexuality. As if heterosexual people have a leg up on sanctification over same-sex-attracted people. But the proper response to homosexuality is not heterosexuality; it's holiness. God does not need to make me, or anyone, heterosexual to make us holy.

These assumptions also introduce an anemic theology of healing and restoration. Now, I'm a dyed-in-the-wool charismatic. I believe the gifts of the Spirit are for today. I've seen miracles and I pray for them. I speak in tongues. When somebody has a prophetic word I sit in attention, filled with anticipation. I hunger for these things. But I have also seen firsthand how belief in supernatural healings and deliverance has led to manipulation, shame, control, and abuse. So, I try to temper my hunger with wisdom. And the way we talk about same-sex attraction and gender dysphoria in the church has often lacked wisdom.

For one, there are no accounts in Scripture of God healing someone's same-sex attraction or gender dysphoria. Not one. In addition, few people are relieved of their fallen desires upon entering union with Christ. They may experience seasons of reprieve, but once salvation loses that "new car smell," many people find themselves returning to sinful patterns. When this happens, they are filled with shame and may wonder if God really saved them in the first place or if he was ever real.

This shame happens for a number of reasons. One is that while many churches take sin seriously, they often fail to take the psychological forces that underpin our sin seriously. We moralize what are often trauma responses, attempted coping solutions, and the ways abuse has formed us. Another reason this shame hinders so deeply is that we misrepresent what the Bible means by restoration.

As I've already mentioned, one of the great joys of my vocation is helping Christians think biblically and lovingly through the topic of their LGBTQ+ neighbors and the church. Whenever I travel to speak or hop on a Zoom call, I am always asked what books I would recommend people read for further study. Of course, *People to Be Loved* and *Embodied* by Preston Sprinkle get shout-outs every time.[5] *Single, Gay, Christian* by Gregory Coles and *War of Loves* by David Bennett are exemplary reads.[6] But if there was one book I could get into everybody's hands in our quest to be ministers of reconciliation and barrier removers, it would be *Still Time to Care* by Greg Johnson.[7]

In this book Johnson, a pastor by trade and theologian by training, wears the hat of a historian. He examines the broadly failed conversion therapy or reparative therapy movement over the years. In the late '80s and through the '00s, large ministries made the bold claim that through deliverance-style prayer, the study and application of Scripture, and the right type of therapy, homosexual desires could be eliminated. Of course, most of the people who claimed to have been cured by said ministries are now living in queer relationships and have recanted their claims.[8]

Johnson contends that approaching LGBTQ+ orientation with a paradigm of cure has not been helpful or successful.[9] What we need is a paradigm of care. A paradigm of care is rooted in the footwashing, radical love of Jesus that has room for suffering and faithfulness in spite of difficulty. A paradigm of cure is rooted in deeply problematic beliefs about God and holiness.

Conversion therapy (the paradigm of cure), particularly in its more coercive or spiritually manipulative forms, often reflects a kind of prosperity gospel thinking—not in terms of wealth or success but in its transactional view of God. The prosperity gospel reduces the mystery and dynamism of God into a generic formula: "If I do *x*, God will do *y*."

It subtly communicates that if someone truly believes in Jesus, prays hard enough, or submits deeply enough, their unwanted same-sex attraction or gender dysphoria will be removed as God's blessing on them. In this framework, change is not just hoped for but expected, and if it doesn't happen, the fault lies with the person's lack of faith, obedience, or inner healing. This mirrors the prosperity gospel's message: If you have enough faith, you'll be healthy, happy, and successful—and if you're not, it's probably your fault.

This belief system undermines a biblical theology of suffering. Scripture never promises the removal of all our struggles in this life; in fact, it assures us that suffering will be part of our journey (John 16:33; Romans 8:17; Philippians 1:29). The Christian life is not marked by total victory over earthly weakness but by communion with Christ in the midst of our weakness (2 Corinthians 12:9-10). When we teach LGBTQ+ individuals that change is the necessary proof of sanctification or salvation, we not only misrepresent what the gospel offers, but we burden people with false hope and shame. We imply that real faith leads to heterosexuality or gender conformity, as if those were fruits of the Spirit.

The New Testament offers a different vision: one in which some thorns remain, even after prayer, and where spiritual maturity looks like faithfulness in weakness, not the absence of weakness. A robust theology of suffering invites LGBTQ+ people into a deeper, more honest walk with Christ—one that does not equate holiness with heterosexuality but emphasizes growing in trust and communion with a Savior who bore scars and did not promise ease. Instead of demanding change as proof of God's work, the church ought to walk with people patiently, honoring their journey and holding space for both grace and groaning in the already-and-not-yet kingdom of God.

In *Still Time to Care*, Johnson not only conducts a thorough historical analysis of the conversion therapy movement, but he names several prominent evangelical leaders who embraced a posture of care for their queer neighbors, one of those being C. S. Lewis.[10] Being the good Protestant I am, I love Lewis. So I had to dive deeper.

Before the culture wars taught evangelicals to become adversarial toward gay people, Lewis showed hospitality, kindness, and love to his friend Arthur, a gay man. Lewis wrote that after his brother, Arthur was his most intimate friend.[11] He even lent his voice to the movement that sought to decriminalize homosexuality out of his love for Arthur.[12]

Lewis managed to cast a positive vision for same-sex-attracted Christians and their contribution to the church, seeing a potential vocation in their experience. He certainly believed same-sex sexual behavior was sin, but he had a bigger vision for queer people than one of change, fear, and hiding. Lewis writes:

> The disciples were not told why (in terms of efficient cause) the man was born blind (John 9:1-3): only the final cause, that the works of God should be made manifest in him. This suggests that in homosexuality, as in every other tribulation, those works can be made manifest: i.e., that every disability conceals a vocation, if only we find it, which would "turn the necessity to glorious gain."[13]

In a moment when it was criminal to be gay, when fear and suspicion of queer people were as high as ever, Lewis modeled a Christlike way forward. Rather than viewing queer people as adversaries, he viewed them as people to be loved. He also dared to believe they had a unique contribution to make to the body of Christ: a contribution that could not and would not be made if they were required to hide, leave, or pretend to have their orientations changed.

INAUGURATED ESCHATOLOGY

Jesus loves to surprise us and catch us off guard. This is how Jesus topples empires—not through violence, coercion, cruelty, or marginalizing people but by loving and serving the ones empires crush. Repeatedly in the Gospels we see Jesus reach beyond barriers to love people into wholeness. These were people the social and religious customs of his day told him he should not associate with: the Samaritan woman at the well, five times divorced and shacking up with her boyfriend (John 4:1-26). The woman caught red-handed in adultery (John 8:1-11). The lepers he spoke to and touched, who were the most severely marginalized members of society by far (Matthew 8:1-4; Mark 1:40-45; Luke 17:11-19). And now this blind man in Luke 18. Removing barriers is key to practicing the way of Jesus.

We live in what many theologians call an "inaugurated eschatology." Let's be honest: Theologians love fancy words the way cats love cardboard boxes—nobody really knows why, but they just can't stay out of them. Let me briefly break down what this phrase means. It is quite beautiful once you peel off the layers of syllables.

Eschatology is the study of the last things (from the Greek *eschatos*, meaning "last" or "final"). If something is inaugurated, it's been launched but not yet completed. So inaugurated eschatology is the belief that God's final work of renewal has already begun in Jesus but won't be fully complete until his return. It's the tension of living in the already and the not yet.

Put another way, Christ's first coming inaugurated the reign of God, but we await his second coming for the fullness of that kingdom. This framework, rooted in the teachings of Jesus and the writings of Paul, helps us understand why restoration and healing are present but not complete in this age. Jesus proclaimed that the kingdom of God had come near (Mark 1:15), and his miracles—healing the sick, forgiving sins, restoring the marginalized—were signs of that inbreaking power (Luke 7:22). Yet Paul acknowledges that creation still "groans" as it awaits full redemption (Romans 8:22-23). Inaugurated eschatology affirms that real transformation is possible now, but full restoration belongs to the age to come. This tension protects us from both utopian overreach and cynical resignation.

When applied to complex issues like LGBTQ+ orientation and the hope of healing or transformation, inaugurated eschatology offers a more biblically faithful posture than either triumphalism or despair. The New Testament does not promise the elimination of every experience of brokenness in this life. Rather, it assures us that our identities and longings are being reshaped in Christ as we await our full redemption (1 Corinthians 6:11; Philippians 3:20-21). Thus, many of us may walk faithfully with unfulfilled longings, trusting that the coming kingdom will bring final healing. As one scholar wrote, "The Church is a community of eschatological hope . . . where God's future is already being lived out, however incompletely."[14] In this light, discipleship for LGBTQ+ believers is not contingent on immediate change but on faithful perseverance in the hope of full restoration.

REFLECTION QUESTIONS

1. How can Jesus' example of crossing social and religious barriers shape the way we relate to LGBTQ+ people today?
2. How can the church encourage LGBTQ+ believers to persevere faithfully, even when their longings or struggles remain unresolved?
3. How might Jesus' surprising love challenge your own assumptions or fears about reaching out to your LGBTQ+ neighbors?

7

REPENT AND BELIEVE

If my sinfulness appears to me in any way smaller or less detestable in comparison with the sins of others, I am not recognizing my sins at all.

Dietrich Bonhoeffer

Max Lucado might be the most prolific living pastor in America. His trademark warmth and edifying style have been a source of comfort and inspiration for millions of Christians throughout the decades. But 2004 saw a rare moment in which Lucado traded his normal warmth for something more biting. While addressing the topic of homosexuality, Lucado used uncharacteristically alarmist language, saying, "How will homosexuality impact our culture? What about the spread of disease? If gay lifestyle and gay marriage is endorsed—what follows? Polygamy? Legalized incest? If we can't draw a line, will lines be drawn at all?"[1]

To be clear, the issue with Lucado's words is not his belief in traditional marriage but his lack of compassion and psychological nuance. It is never helpful to compare same-sex activity or desire to other forms of sexual expression that lead to abuse and lasting harm. These words resurfaced in 2021, and Lucado faced a public outcry related to the harsh language.

How did Lucado respond? He could have ignored the pushback, refusing to acknowledge words from a sermon preached fifteen years earlier. Or he could have dug his heels in, rallied the culture warriors who would have gladly come to his aid, and fought the complaints. After all, few American pastors have the resources and influence Lucado has.

But he chose neither of those options, instead taking a third path. He repented. Lucado issued the following apology in a public statement:

> In 2004 I preached a sermon on the topic of same-sex marriage. I now see that, in that sermon, I was disrespectful. I was hurtful. I wounded people in ways that were devastating. I should have done better. It grieves me that my words have hurt or been used to hurt the LGBTQ community. I apologize to you and I ask forgiveness of Christ.
>
> Faithful people may disagree about what the Bible says about homosexuality, but we agree that God's holy Word must never be used as a weapon to wound others. To be clear, I believe in the traditional biblical understanding of marriage, but I also believe in a God of unbounded grace and love. LGBTQ individuals and LGBTQ families must be respected and treated with love. They are beloved children of God because they are made in the image and likeness of God.
>
> Over centuries, the church has harmed LGBTQ people and their families, just as the church has harmed people

> on issues of race, gender, divorce, addiction, and so many other things. We must do better to serve and love one another.[2]

These words bring tears to my eyes. Rather than mirroring the anxiety and reactivity so common in public evangelical responses to LGBTQ+ people, Lucado responded in contrition. He took accountability, named the wrongdoing, and provoked his readers to a deepening of empathy for the people he had hurt.

In repenting, Lucado invited anyone who took his words with weight to do likewise. And when we repent we're one step closer to the kingdom of God.

SAYING EVERYTHING WITH JUST A FEW WORDS

Repentance was at the heart of the first sermon Jesus preached: "After John was put in prison, Jesus went into Galilee, proclaiming the good news of God. 'The time has come,' he said. 'The kingdom of God has come near. Repent and believe the good news!'" (Mark 1:14-15).

This sermon is both simple and packs a punch. We can break it down into two basic ideas: One, the kingdom of God is near. Two, repent and believe the gospel.

If we're serious about following Jesus, we need to root our conversation in something deeper than cultural trends or personal intuitions about what feels loving. To discern a Christlike path, especially in such a tender and complex area, we need to return to the core of the gospel message: belief and repentance. Not just for our LGBTQ+ neighbors but for us—for the church.

The kingdom of God is near. We can boil down pretty much everything Jesus said and did to announcing, demonstrating, and inviting people into the kingdom of God. The first words of this sermon are, "The kingdom of God has come near." Jesus also instructs his disciples to pray, "Your kingdom come" (Matthew 6:10). If the kingdom of God is near, and we are to pray for it to come, then it is not an ethereal realm we gain access to "some bright morning when this life is o'er," as the classic hymn would indicate. The kingdom of God is much nearer than that.

This raises a central question: What *is* the kingdom of God? Is it a government, a new political system, a dictatorship, a monarchy? The word *kingdom* often evokes associations with conquest, dominance, and oppression. Is this kingdom forceful, violent, or coercive? If so, then maybe the church has represented the kingdom of God accurately when it's been cruel or violent, not just to LGBTQ+ people but to anyone.

But these troubling associations with the word *kingdom* do not paint an accurate picture of what Jesus means when he talks about the kingdom of God. And the best of New Testament scholarship backs this claim[3]. If Jesus' words and deeds were an announcement, a demonstration, an open invitation, then the kingdom he brings is nothing like our kingdoms. Not empire, not democracy, not republic. It is wild, upside-down, and wholly God's.

When we look at Jesus, we see what life lived in this kingdom looks like. We see that this is a kingdom where beggars are offered the seat of honor at fancy banquets. It is a kingdom where outcasts are included and arrogant religious types are scolded. It is a kingdom where the dirty and the left out receive grand invitations. It is a kingdom where the poor receive good news, the blind receive sight, those held in bondage and oppression are set free, and the Lord's favor is withheld from no one. It is a kingdom of peace, forgiveness, justice, holiness, truth, and beauty. It is a kingdom with a feast table big enough for all our stories, no matter how messy. It is a kingdom where everything is as it was meant to be.

The kingdom of God is here and now, and it is not yet.

This means we are to live our lives considering this kingdom. Our goal is that the kingdom of God would become the content and context of our very lives. Just as God's will was done in and through Jesus, God's will ought to be done in and through us. It's not easy, and of course we will fail repeatedly. Even so, kingdom living is the North Star for any follower of Jesus. We are called to live in this present age as if we are living in the age to come. Jewish scholar Amy-Jill Levine writes, "When Jesus talks about the Kingdom of Heaven, he invites his followers into a radical reorientation—toward compassion, justice, and communal responsibility. It's not a reward system—it's a summons to live differently now."[4]

Repent and believe the good news. The reality of this kingdom does not come about by willpower or adjusting one's thinking. Entering into this new way of living requires belief in the one who creates the path for us. And this belief is not as simple as accepting it as true.

In our post-Enlightenment world, we tend to place the highest authority on mental assent. Get your thinking right and that's all that matters. The way the New Testament writers talk about belief is far more holistic, risky, and transgressive than that.

The Greek word translated "believe" in Jesus' call to "repent and believe the good news" is *pisteuō*, a variation of the Greek *pistis*. Theologian Matthew Bates puts it succinctly: "The Greek word *pistis*, generally rendered 'faith' or 'belief,' as it pertains to

Christian salvation, quite simply has little correlation with 'faith' and 'belief' as these words are generally understood and used in contemporary Christian culture, and much to do with allegiance. . . . Properly speaking, *pistis* is not part of the gospel but the only fitting response to the gospel."[5]

In Scripture, faith isn't just believing the right ideas, it's reorienting your entire life toward God. Think of it this way: belief + faithfulness + allegiance = New Testament faith. When Jesus announces that the kingdom of heaven is near, he's not calling for mental assent; he's calling for total surrender—our minds, our wills, our loyalties.

But to enter this kingdom, we must first repent. Repent of our warped thinking. Repent of our self-serving actions. Repent of our misplaced allegiances.

Words like *sin* and *repentance* may sound outdated, but they name the heart of the human struggle. Ignore them, and we strip ourselves of the language to describe our brokenness—and the map to find our way home.

Sin is both a condition we inherit and the decisions we make. We are both victims and perpetrators of sin. Sin is the great equalizer in humanity. No matter how much money we do or do not have, no matter how popular or ignored, no matter how noble or sinister, we are all, every one of us, infected and affected by sin.

It is possible to have your soul saved by Jesus and still live in a system shaped by Satan. From the lingering effects of systemic racism in the United States to the husband who cheats on his wife. From the gas chambers in Auschwitz to the person who hoards their wealth—all of it is sin. All of it is an attempt to live our lives on our own terms, apart from the love of God.

Here's why I'm spending so much ink on the kingdom, belief, and repentance: Sin runs deep. It would be naive—maybe even foolish—to think the church's treatment of LGBTQ+ people hasn't been tainted by it. And the only way out of sin is through repentance. When we think of repentance, it's easy to conjure an image of a hellfire-and-brimstone preacher yelling at us to "turn or burn!" But in the Bible, repentance simply means "turn around." Far from being shameful, repentance is one of the most beautiful concepts in all of Scripture. It means that when we have wandered off course or missed the mark, all we have to do is turn around and greet the kindness of Jesus waiting for us.

Jesus' first sermon demonstrates that we do not have the resources to bring this new creation to bear on our own. The world, our culture, and our best human innovations do not have what it takes to restore flawed and weary souls. We need to repent of our ways. We need to turn around. We need to surrender our meager way of life and take on the Jesus way of life.

As we do, we commit ourselves in lifelong covenant to Jesus and his way. We devote the rest of our lives to laying down our old selves, the selves marked by death and decay, and we take on a Jesus-shaped new self. We devote our lives to dwelling with our Creator, being transformed into his likeness, and mirroring his goodness to the world.

If we do not embrace this heart disposition and sanctified behavior, we are not recognizably Christian. Jesus' message ought to permeate every area of our lives as nothing in our hearts, minds, or bodies goes untouched by Jesus.

Believing in the gospel means we see people with the eyes of Jesus, human beings worthy of our love, our service, and our repentance. When Christians allow themselves to see LGBTQ+ people as more than a political talking point or enemy in a culture war, we will be humbled by the divine image they carry and convicted for the ways they have been treated as less than the *imago Dei*.

A FEARLESS MORAL INVENTORY

Despite our agreement with Jesus' first sermon, many of us get defensive the moment someone tells us to repent. I see it in others, and I see it in myself. It's a strange reaction, isn't it? You'd think followers of Jesus—the One who calls us to repentance—would welcome every chance to turn closer to him.

If we really believe sin still clings to us, if we know blind spots exist in our character, then repentance should be second nature. But it's not. Most of us repented once, back when we first came to faith, and maybe we repent of the sins that weigh heavy on our conscience. But let someone else name our sin, and we're ready for a fight. I know I am.

I am fortunate to frequently find myself in the room while pastors and Christian leaders are looking for resources on how to navigate LGBTQ+ topics and the church. Often what they seek first is a proper theological position, an intro to the terminology, the ethics of addressing people by their chosen pronouns, whether it's okay to attend a gay wedding, and what to do if a LGBTQ+ person wants to join the worship team. What I don't see mentioned as often is the sin Christians have inflicted on our LGBTQ+ neighbors and how that has shaped the moment we live in.

Repentance is key to addressing the church's sordid history with LGBTQ+ people. And the gospel is what empowers this repentance.

Due to its Christian origins, the twelve step journey of Alcoholics Anonymous includes a beautiful invitation to step into gospel living. Step three states, "We made the decision to turn our will and our lives over to the care of God." Step four calls addicts to honestly examine their past and acknowledge how it has affected them and their loved ones—to make a "fearless moral inventory."

Here we have a poignant call to repentance: Decide to turn your will and life over to the care of God, and make a searching and fearless moral inventory of yourself. Saint Ignatius of Loyola would call this an examination of the heart. The Psalms invite us to pray for the Lord's help in this practice:

> Search me, God, and know my heart;
>   test me and know my anxious thoughts.
> See if there is any offensive way in me,
>   and lead me in the way everlasting. (Psalm 139:23-24)

If we're serious about joining Jesus in the ministry of reconciliation, we've got to start with a fearless look in the mirror. The church—beautiful, broken, holy, and chaotic as it is—has some confessing to do.

When we pretend there's no tension between the church and the LGBTQ+ community, we forfeit credibility. We lose trust. And those quietly wrestling within our pews learn that the safest place to hide is behind a polite smile and a carefully guarded secret.

Repentance isn't a PR move; it's a spiritual necessity. Without it, we stop growing. Without it, we stop looking like Jesus. Many genuine moves toward holiness begin with the words, "I was wrong."

MERCY AND JUDGMENT

Many today who call themselves Christians are not interested in being Christlike. There is no etymological difference between those terms, *Christian* and *Christlike*. They mean the same thing. To be a Christian should always imply the obsessive pursuit of Christlikeness. There is, however, a significant difference in how we understand these words today. Many Christians have been harsh and inhospitable toward LGBTQ+ Christians, but this can never be Christlike.

Consider James 2. The author, who very well could have been Jesus' little brother, writes this: "Speak and act as those who are going to be judged by the law that gives freedom, because judgment without mercy will be shown to anyone who has not been merciful. Mercy triumphs over judgment" (James 2:12-13).

Under Christ, the law we live by is a law of freedom—not bondage or condemnation. But freedom has a shape. Those who refuse mercy will face judgment without it. Christianity is not "You better not screw up"; it's "My chains fell off." God's heart is that his people would embody mercy. And in his justice, he ensures that mercy wins by holding the merciless accountable.

Charles Spurgeon preached, "God's mercy is so great that you may sooner drain the sea of its water, or deprive the sun of its light, or make space too narrow, than diminish the great mercy of God."[6] And yet far too often when it comes to our LGBTQ+ neighbors, the church has allowed judgment to triumph over mercy.

I have heard folks charitably push back against applying this text to the LGBTQ+ conversation. The fear is that this line of reasoning will lead to tolerance of sin. If the church shows them mercy instead of judgment, it might send the wrong idea about how it feels about their sin. When I hear this, it makes me wonder if people think we aren't tolerating each other's sin, on some level, all the time. It makes me think the person asking assumes people aren't, on some level, tolerating their sins just by being in relationship with them.[7]

Every one of us is a sinner. We carry flaws, dysfunction, and broken ways of being in the world. None of us were perfectly loved, and that lack has shaped us to live selfishly. Some of us are better at disguising it; others have tasted deep healing through the Spirit of God. But all of us bear the marks of sin—and all of us have the power to pass that brokenness on.

To live in community—church, family, friendship—is to constantly make space for one another's unfinished stories. This isn't endorsing sin; it's acknowledging reality. We are works in progress. Some desires fall away the moment we meet Christ. Others we wrestle with for a lifetime. Sanctification is a slow, long obedience in the same direction.[8]

Only those refined by fire—every impurity consumed, every selfish desire gone—could ever claim the right to let judgment eclipse mercy. And yet, those rare souls who come close still choose mercy every time.

Our journey toward Christlikeness would accelerate if we spent less energy condemning others and more energy surrendering our own sin. We magnify the sin we see in others and minimize the sin within us. Scripture does not call us to deny sin's reality but to meet it with mercy.

If we can confess our failure to extend mercy to our LGBTQ+ neighbors, that confession becomes the doorway to repentance.

WHAT DO I HAVE TO REPENT OF?

The inevitable question that arises when we talk about the need for repentance in reconciliation conversations is, "Why should I have to repent? I've never been homophobic or transphobic. Why should I repent of something other Christians have done?"

Charitably, this question comes from someone who has done a searching and fearless moral inventory and genuinely does not feel the need to repent. Cynically, the inquirer feels defensive at the prospect of being asked to repent for anything, guilty or not. Often defensiveness blocks our ability to seriously evaluate ourselves.

But let's say you genuinely do not believe you have been unjust or harsh toward queer people, that you do not see what you have to repent of. You are not alone in feeling that way. And I don't judge you for that. I would simply invite you to consider a wider perspective of what repentance is. Many of us assume repentance is strictly an individualistic act, between us and God only. Many of us do not have a category for corporate or communal repentance. So when we hear things like "the church needs to repent," it strikes us as disingenuous.

However, this personal understanding of repentance is shaped more by what Charles Taylor calls "expressive individualism" than by a biblical imagination. Expressive individualism is the idea that each of us has a unique way of curating our identity and we are called to live that out (express it) rather than conform it to models imposed on us by others (family, country, religion, church, Scripture). Elaborating on this idea, Taylor writes, "There is a certain way of being human that is my way. I am called upon to live my life in this way. . . . If I am not true to myself, I miss the point of my life. This notion gives a new importance to being true to myself. Being true to myself means being true to my own originality."[9]

It is hard to overstate the impact expressive individualism has had on how we read the Bible, how we follow Jesus, how we see ourselves and others, and how we think about repentance. To properly understand why communal repentance might be so difficult to wrap our minds around, we have to understand this era of expressive individualism.

THE SOVEREIGN SELF

The focal point of Western individualism is the self. Essentially, the self is the "real you." What makes you the real you? How you answer that question today is likely quite different from how you would have answered it five hundred years ago.

In centuries past a person found a sense of self (or identity) not as a fully expressed individual but as a contributing member of a community. In fact, one's identity was viewed as a shared identity, and this was often at the expense and well-being of the individual. The societal pressure of centuries past was not "you be you" but severe conformity for the sake of the whole. One found identity from an outside source—a tribe, a family, a religion, God, the gods, Scripture—and the highest good one could aspire to was to live into the identity defined by the outside source.

As Dr. Christopher Watkin observes, "Why do pre-Renaissance portraits make little effort to represent the distinctive features of the individual? Why, for that matter, are there relatively few pre-Renaissance portraits of living individuals? The reason, in part, is that the individual mattered relatively little; the social structure was of prime importance."[10]

By contrast, today we seek to be authentic individuals, even if that comes at the expense of our communities' well-being. There are many names for this newer phenomenon. Charles Taylor calls it "expressive individualism," while Carl Trueman calls it "the modern self." Trueman writes, "The modern self sees the authority of inner feelings, and sees authenticity as the ability to give social expression to do the same. The modern self also assumes that society at large will recognize and affirm such behavior."[11]

Today, being "fully realized" means living out our feelings without restraint. The modern Western ideal crowns the sovereign self—free from religion, family, and nation. Liberation is measured by how untethered we are from any tradition that might shape, challenge, or restrain our desires.

In the Christian worldview, we are neither simply pieces of a whole nor merely isolated individuals. Christianity affirms both our need for community and the God-given uniqueness of each person.

The Trinity models this beautifully: three distinct persons—Father, Son, and Holy Spirit inseparable yet unique. Likewise, we are called to live as parts of a collective while honoring our individual contributions. As Paul writes, "You are the body of Christ, and each one of you is a part of it" (1 Corinthians 12:27).

When the church is invited to communal repentance for its treatment of LGBTQ+ neighbors, we are called to understand repentance with this biblical imagination, not through the lens of expressive individualism.

THE BIBLE AND COMMUNAL REPENTANCE VERSUS INDIVIDUAL REPENTANCE

Scripture talks about our relationship with God in communal terms more frequently than in individualistic terms. God's covenant with Abraham started with an individual but was destined to become communal in nature (Genesis 12:1-3). This is the Old Testament pattern; what starts as God's covenant with one person grows into God's covenant with a nation. In the New Testament, almost all of Paul's letters are written to churches, not one or two specific people (unless he specifies otherwise). When we read Ephesians or either of the Corinthians for our devotional time, it's easy to think Paul's "you" is directed at us as individuals. But the original recipients of his letters would not have thought that.

Most of Paul's letters were addressed to a specific church (e.g., "To God's holy people in Colossae," Colossians 1:2). The letters were then read to the assembly of Christians in that region. They were not read by individuals sitting alone with coffee listening to low-fi worship beats during their quiet time. When the original audience heard the New Testament letters read aloud and heard the word "you," they would have seen a room full of sinners and saints all listening to the same words. The "you" is plural, not singular. Our brothers and sisters in the American South can help us understand this with their popular "y'all."

It's easy to project our current moment's high value for individualism onto Scripture, and how we do church in the West often reinforces this error. It's not uncommon for church ministry to feel like a buffet—we pick what we put on your plate to suit our needs. We have kids' ministries, youth ministries, men's ministries, women's ministries, divorced groups, singles groups, marriage groups, "prime-timers" groups, and cycling groups.

There's nothing wrong with gathering with people like you, but it can feed the idea that faith is purely personal—a private transaction between you and Jesus. Scripture, however, paints a different picture: The church is one body, interdependent and alive together. As I've heard it said, "Christ is coming back for a bride, not a harem."

Of course, we do have our own personal relationship with God, as Jesus demonstrates with his teaching on the secret place (Matthew 6:6-7), but we also relate to God communally. It's not an either-or; it's a both/and. When you step into relationship with Jesus you also step into community with all the people who call him Lord. The good, the bad, and the ugly. If this is true, then our repentance must be both individual and communal.

There are several biblical examples that illustrate the call for communal repentance, but let's look at just two from the Old Testament. Isaiah writes:

> Wash and make yourselves clean.
>   Take your evil deeds out of my sight;
>   stop doing wrong.
> Learn to do right; seek justice.
>   Defend the oppressed.
> Take up the cause of the fatherless;
>   plead the case of the widow. (Isaiah 1:16-17)

This is an address to the whole nation of Israel, not just a king, general, social elite, or farmer who worshiped the idol Baal. It is not a call for a specific individual to repent but for the whole of Israel, including the ones who may think they've done nothing wrong.

Because God's covenant was with the whole nation, the whole nation is held to account. All Israel was culpable in failing to do right, seek justice, defend the oppressed, take up the cause of the fatherless, and plead the case of the widow. And because the whole nation was culpable, the Lord through Isaiah invites the whole nation to repent.

Even more pointedly, let's look at the book of Daniel:

> So I turned to the Lord God and pleaded with him in prayer and petition, in fasting, and in sackcloth and ashes.
>
> I prayed to the LORD my God and confessed:
>
> > "Lord, the great and awesome God, who keeps his covenant of love with those who love him and keep his commandments, we have sinned and done wrong. We have been wicked and have rebelled; we have turned away from your commands and laws. We have not listened to your servants the prophets, who spoke in your name to our kings, our princes and our ancestors, and to all the people of the land." (Daniel 9:3-6)

Daniel is not simply crying out to the Lord and repenting of his own sin, although that is absolutely a worthwhile practice for us to adopt. Daniel is crying out and repenting on behalf of his people. What's wild about this prayer is that Daniel may be the least culpable Israelite in the whole nation. Daniel is radically consecrated unto the Lord. His whole story is one of sweeping fidelity in an age of compromise.

When we look carefully at the life of Daniel, we do not see that he is guilty of the things he's repenting of on behalf of Israel. He is a captive in Babylon because of his nation's choices, not his own. Yet Daniel does not see himself as separate from his nation. He is one with them, a part of Israel's communal covenant with the Lord. And so, even though he may not have committed the sins he is repenting of, Daniel still repents.

Similarly, we are a part of the church's communal covenant with God. When the church sins, it's not just a few bad apples a long time ago or some whack-job pastor in another state. Christ prayed for us to be one as he and the Father are one. Because of this, God looks at us as one. We are his bride, not his brides. We are his body, not his bodies.

So when the church sins against LGBTQ+ people, the church as a whole must repent. Repentance is the only appropriate response to sin. In the next chapter, we'll explore what this repentance can look like in our churches.

WHAT IF I'VE BEEN HURT BY THE LGBTQ+ COMMUNITY?

Getting to be on the front lines of helping Christians think theologically and lovingly about these things has been one of my life's biggest blessings. Because I am positioned to love and serve the people I pastor, the church leaders I connect with, and members of the LGBTQ+ community, I know the pain that often accompanies this conversation cuts both ways.

I have sat with husbands as they sobbed in my living room because their wives wanted to embrace a queer identity and compromise fidelity in their marriage. In one scenario, a wife left her husband to pursue relationships with women. In another, the wife gave her husband an ultimatum: agree to a polyamorous marriage in which she could explore her sexuality with other women, or get a divorce.

I have sat with fathers and mothers as they described discerning their children's names with prayer, believing the act of naming their child was holy and prophetic. I have seen them weep after those children came out as trans and hosted "dead-naming" ceremonies, a ritual in which a trans person rejects their given name and takes a new one. I have sat with pastors who have faithfully loved and served members of their church—dedicating them as babies, baptizing them, performing their weddings—only to later be accused by those same people of hate and bigotry because they disagreed on sexual ethics.

No matter who you are or what the cause, rejection and abandonment are agonizingly painful.

No, these examples are not the same as some of the violence, bigotry, fear, and hate many LGBTQ+ people have experienced in church. But this is real pain, real baggage, real cause for apprehension, and these are common reasons to resist repentance in this area. Some folks who have gone through similar experiences may be bewildered when it comes to this conversation. They may feel like they don't have a lot of wind in their sails to help make church a place where LGBTQ+ Christians can encounter the real Jesus. And honestly, who can blame them?

This is where I see the Lord inviting us in and through our pain. It is important and healthy to name our pain, to process it, and to grieve it. Not every feeling needs expression, but every feeling does need recognition. It is appropriate to be angry at injustices we have suffered and to mourn relationships that have changed.

We must grieve and heal in order to move forward. Our spiritual and psychological well-being depends on it. And we grieve knowing God weeps with us. But just as experiencing same-sex attraction does not give someone like me an excuse to bend historic Christian theology to my desires, pain does not give us license to ignore what God has called us to.

The pain we endure does not remove the calling on our lives. If anything, it makes us more effective when we step into it. We are still called to love and embrace our neighbor as we have been loved and embraced by Christ. We are still charged with the commission to invite hurting, broken, flawed people to the feet of Jesus. We are still ambassadors of heaven, co-laborers with Christ in the ministry of reconciliation. When we or the spiritual family we call church falls short, we are still called to repent. If we are going to invite anyone to repentance, we have to model it first.

To do that, we have to make a searching and fearless moral inventory. We have to courageously examine where we have fallen short and how we can do better. Not to appeal to some progressive ideology. Not as a cynical form of virtue signaling. And not as a church-growth strategy. But because we are called to do so by the author and perfecter of our faith, and our own spiritual maturity depends on it. We repent because it is the only proper response to a revelation of Christ's love.

We can't change the fact that there will always be a Dillon Awes with vile things to say that misrepresent Christ in infuriating ways. We can't change our history. But through repentance we can help to form our churches into communities that bear witness to the life, light, and love of Jesus. And in our bearing witness, we can contradict headline-making, hate-filled rhetoric in a manner that is full of hope.

REFLECTION QUESTIONS

1. What's the difference between individual repentance and communal repentance in Scripture? Why does it matter?
2. Where has the church historically failed LGBTQ+ people, and what would it look like to name that honestly?
3. Why is repentance so often mistaken for compromise? What does true, biblical repentance actually lead to?

8

THE FRUITS OF REPENTANCE

Peacemaking is not a side project of the gospel. It is the gospel—the good news that enemies can be friends, the lost can be found, and even death doesn't get the last word.

Melissa Florer-Bixler

If we take Jesus' call to corporate and individual repentance seriously, our churches will start to look and sound different. Let's look at how we can intentionally live out the love of Jesus and redeem our witness to our LGTBQ+ neighbors.

MODEL IT IN OUR TEACHING

The Bible tells a beautiful story of what sex is for, what marriage is, and why our bodies matter. And the world is also telling a story—one that does not lead to human flourishing by any discernible metric. Just look at the mental health crisis our culture is experiencing.

We have a better story of sex, marriage, intimacy, and the body than the world does, and we need to disciple our people into that story. If we do not, the world will gladly step in and do it for us.

Inevitably, if churches are going to teach people about sex, marriage, and the human body, and if we want to speak to the world our people actually live in, we have to address homosexuality and gender dysphoria. When we do this, we absolutely must name the ways the church has done this badly. I'm not saying we need to get theatrical or resort to virtue signaling. But I am saying we need to name the destructive ways churches have treated LGBTQ+ people, and we need to name what it has cost. It has cost the church its witness, not just to our LGBTQ+ neighbors but to others as well. It has cost family members opportunities to love and serve their queer loved ones. And in some cases it has cost the lives of LGBTQ+ people, either via suicide or hate crimes.

It doesn't do anyone any favors to act like ostriches with our heads in the sand, pretending we don't know how tumultuous church has been for LGBTQ+ people. Naming our history provides a better path forward. It empowers us to teach Scripture in a manner that is full of grace, truth, and repentance. It teaches our families and communities that the only proper response to sin of any kind is repentance.

But most of all, it shows people who experience same-sex attraction or gender dysphoria, or who love someone on that journey, that our church is a safe place for them to find and follow Jesus. And that right there is the heart of this conversation. We want anyone and everyone to have the opportunity to experience Christ in community. Christ's table is big enough for all our stories, no matter how messy or complicated.

There are plenty of reasons someone might not want to follow Jesus, so let's make sure Christian behavior on these topics isn't one of them. When we talk about our sordid history up front, in a way that unapologetically denounces the worst moments of our history toward queer people without downplaying the wisdom of Scripture, we begin to create a culture with one less barrier for people to overcome in order to find and follow Jesus.

LET YOUR HEART BE MOVED

A few years ago I shared my story at a conference in Boise, Idaho. Afterward, as I was talking with people and shaking hands, a gentleman approached me with tears in his eyes.

He said, "Tony, there have been moments in my life when I was the guy people like you needed to be afraid of. I was the one who called gay people the moral disease of our country. I was the one who made homophobic jokes. I was the one who didn't want you in my church." The man's tears turned to quiet sobs, and he said, "I am so sorry. I am so, so sorry."

He asked if he could hug me, and we did, and he sobbed a little more. I began to weep too. And something miraculous happened. His tears, his repentance, in a mysterious way healed some lingering wounds in my own soul. I had shared my journey from the stage several times before this interaction, and each time people were sympathetic, but I was unconvinced my story was doing anything other than garnering sympathy. I am allergic to pity. I want to share my story only if it will help people draw closer to Jesus.

After this experience, my cynicism turned to hope. Hope that this man's heart was changing, that my heart was changing, and that church could actually be a place where the real-deal presence of Christ could be encountered by anyone curious enough to seek him out. What a thought.

If you hear a story from someone in church who has wrestled with same-sex desires or gender dysphoria, allow your heart to be moved. Suspend for a moment the urge to have the right doctrine or make sure they have the right doctrine. Listen attentively and let empathy fill your heart. Remember that the person sharing is not your enemy but your neighbor. No matter who we are, our stories are the sacred manuscripts the Lord writes on. When we behold someone's story, we behold something sacred. And when we behold something sacred, it's good and proper to let it move our hearts.

KNOW YOUR CONTEXT

Of course, I do not know your personal context. What repentance looks like for Christians in Portland, Oregon, might be far different from what it looks like for Christians in Charlotte, North Carolina. So listen, learn, read the Scriptures diligently, and develop your ear to the guidance of the Holy Spirit. What is an earnest way for your church to model repentance when discussing your LGBTQ+ neighbors?

A pastor friend in Los Angeles hands out water bottles at Pride parades, showing that repentance is more than words—it's love in motion. A simple gesture, yet it whispers, "You matter. You are seen."

In Pennsylvania, another pastor invites speakers living with same-sex attraction to share their stories, creating space for hearts to soften and for congregants to engage in the moral inventory we explored earlier.

I know families teaching their children both the beauty of God's design for marriage and the empathy to recognize how the church has often failed to communicate it with love.

We do not have to compromise grace for truth. Anytime we do compromise grace in telling the truth, we no longer view the truth as God does and may even have departed from it. To tell the truth without grace is to reveal we don't see the truth as clearly as we thought. As one writer puts it, "Truth without grace leads to hypocrisy and self-righteousness. Grace without truth leads to moral indifference."[1]

Whatever your context, be intentional about observing what repentance could look like. Remember, the goal isn't to engage in cynical virtue signaling. The goal isn't to grow a church. The goal isn't to appease progressives or play into the cultural script.

The goal is twofold: First, the only proper response to sin is repentance. Second, if we want to remove barriers for our LGBTQ+ neighbors both inside and outside of the church, if we want to help them find and follow Jesus, we must live out the fruits of repentance in our everyday spaces.

LIVE AS PEACEMAKERS

In chapter five we examined Murray Bowen's family systems theory and Edwin Friedman's adaptation of that theory to reveal cycles of anxiety. The only way families and communities can break out of this vicious cycle is to insert a "non-anxious presence" right in the middle of it all. A non-anxious presence is someone who does not "catch" anxiety when it is thrown at them. Instead, they are committed to managing and defusing anxiety.

This work cannot be overlooked. Recently during a Sunday morning service in the church I serve, a few key staff members were out and we were short on some critical volunteers. This meant several of us had to pick up the slack. It did not take long for those who were feeling the anxiety to start spreading it to others like the flu. But when the anxiety reached our non-anxious teammates, they calmly defused the situation.

The subject of LGBTQ+ people and the church is fraught with anxiety and outrage. How can Christians engage this chronically anxious conversation without catching all the anxiety embedded in it? We do it by depending on God for our well-being—not cultural influence, not power, not politicians, and not our best theological defenses.

Jesus had a term for what Friedman calls a non-anxious presence. Jesus called these people peacemakers. And peacemakers are blessed (Matthew 5:9). The word for "blessed" in the original Greek can also be translated as "happy."

Have you ever noticed how deeply unhappy and unpleasant culture warriors tend to be? If you find yourself sucked into the rabbit hole of ideological warfare, you know how it drains you of joy like a bucket full of water with a massive hole in it. But the people who have made the cultivation of peace their mission are among the most joyful.

When Christians take up arms in the culture war we lose a sense of our God-given vocation. We make enemies of people we are called to love. We alienate rather than reconcile. We become ambassadors of a culture fueled by human anxiety rather than ambassadors of heaven fueled by the Spirit of God.

What's more, we erect a barrier between Christ's church, and our LGBTQ+ neighbors. In a culture as anxious as ours, spiritual hunger is rampant. The church carries within it the nourishment spiritually famished people need. Our LGBTQ+ neighbors outside the church are starved for the love, healing, and redemption found in Jesus. We are called to freely give that which we have freely received from Christ.

Furthermore, let us not forget about the faithful remnant of LGBTQ+, same-sex-attracted, and gender-dysphoric people in our pews. What often gets lost in our ideological warring over gender and sexuality is the very real fact that, for thousands upon thousands of people in our churches, this is not a topic to be debated but a lived experience. We have an ecclesiological responsibility to the people we take Communion with. Gay, straight, divorced, addicted, ashamed, depressed, or spiritually wounded, when we are in church we are all limping our way toward Christ together.

The early years of my journey with Jesus did not come with a strong emphasis on peacemaking. In fact, the words of Jesus carried less weight than theological formulas and doctrinal certitude. It was an expression of Christianity that prioritized the pragmatics of systematic theology above the radical pursuit of living a life that resembled that of Jesus. We must not separate our theological convictions from our pursuit of following Jesus.

If we are going to take Jesus at his word, peacemaking is central, not peripheral. Famed evangelist John Stott wrote, "Now peacemaking is a divine work. For peace means reconciliation, and God is the author of peace and of reconciliation. . . . It is hardly surprising, therefore, that the particular blessing which attaches to peacemakers is that 'they shall be called sons of God.' For they are seeking to do what their Father has done, loving people with his love."[2]

There is a cost to failing at peacemaking. Jesus told his followers, "Anyone who loves me will obey my teaching. . . . Anyone who does not love me will not obey my teaching" (John 14:23-24). To practice peacemaking is to obey Jesus, which is to love Jesus.

To blatantly ignore our vocation of peacemaking is to blatantly ignore Jesus. And we can't love someone and ignore him at the same time. I do not say any of this to heap shame. Shaming is a cheap, lazy, and ultimately ineffective discipleship tactic. I say this to be honest. Our failure to obey Christ and his teaching is something he takes personally.

Many, many people who have fought in a culture war did so genuinely believing they were fighting for Jesus. But we have often ended up fighting against him. I'm not saying don't vote your conscience when culture-war issues are up for a vote. I'm not saying be an ostrich with your head in the sand, ignoring the pertinent issues of our time. I am saying that we do everything as apprentices of Jesus, which means we approach life not as soldiers in a war but as practitioners of peace.

The more glued we are to the culture war against our LGBTQ+ neighbors, the more likely we are to assume we know the story of every gay or trans person we come across. We've read the headlines, seen the social media posts, and watched the news. It's easy to fool ourselves into thinking our familiarity with a headline, policy, or movement permits us to bypass knowing a person.

So when we do meet a gay or trans person, we tend to throw curiosity out the window. We've already been told what we need to think about LGBTQ+ people, so we don't need to hear from them. But if we can sit, listen, and learn from them before we tell them how they ought to live, we go much further in our call to become peacemakers.

There's a word for Christians who forsake the words of Jesus while telling others how to live. The word is *hypocrite*. This hypocrisy emits a gnarly stench, not just to LGBTQ+ people but to anyone with a nose to smell.

However, if hypocrisy is a major barrier, the inverse is also true. There is no aroma more appealing to the human soul than a life that mirrors the life of Jesus. If the church's hypocrisy is a barrier for LGBTQ+ people, then wholehearted devotion to Christ-likeness is an enticement. Maybe not to everyone but to anyone aware of their own poverty of spirit and with a hunger for truth.

Anxiety sends a message of calamity. Jesus has a better message, and his is one of life, light, and love. We must stop mixing these messages together. Christ is making an appeal for his message of peace through the church. We are his chosen messengers.

THE PRAYER OF EXAMEN

No practice in the rich history of Christian spiritual formation has aided my quest to become a less-anxious person more than the prayer of examen. This contemplative Christian practice originated with Saint Ignatius of Loyola in the sixteenth century as part of his spiritual exercises, practices that aimed to deepen one's relationship with God through reflection and discernment. Ignatius believed that by examining daily thoughts, emotions, and experiences, one could better recognize the presence of God in all aspects of life and respond accordingly. One author frames it this way: "The Examen is the 'rummaging for God' that allows us to find God's presence even in the clutter of our daily lives."[3]

The examen is traditionally performed in the evening, though many adapt it to suit their schedules. The practice involves five steps:

- ***Remember that you are in God's presence.*** Allow your mind, heart, and body to grow in awareness of his nearness. God is ceaselessly present to you, so take a moment to be present to him. Sometimes I'll slowly repeat the phrase, "Here I am, Lord." Other times I'll recite a breath prayer, saying, "Lord have mercy" as I breathe in and "Christ have mercy" as I breathe out. I'll do this a few times until I sense my awareness of his nearness.
- ***Give thanks for the day.*** Gratitude is key to growing in awareness of God's presence. Our God is so kind, so generous, so loving, that even on the worst days of our lives he gives us reasons to be grateful.
- ***Review the day's events.*** I tend to ask the Holy Spirit to be my guide, not my own obsessions or preoccupations. I have recently been diagnosed with ADHD and can easily get stuck on a particular moment or chase my shiny thoughts until I'm no longer praying. When this happens, I gently return to my breath prayer.
- ***Reflect on emotions and actions that seem significant.*** What feelings stood out to you on this day? What was the cause for these feelings? Did you do anything you need to repent of? Did you sense God speaking or moving in the day?
- ***Look forward to the future with a renewed sense of purpose.*** I end by praying the Lord's Prayer, praying it specifically over my next day.

By pausing to observe our inner life, the examen can help bring clarity to recurring feelings and behaviors, offering an opportunity for greater self-awareness and spiritual growth.

A key benefit of the prayer of examen is its ability to manage and reduce anxiety. By creating space for intentional reflection, the examen helps to slow down racing thoughts and allows for a more thoughtful response to stressors. Instead of letting anxiety build up unexamined, we are encouraged to face fears, frustrations, and insecurities head-on, which often leads to a sense of release and relief.

As we practice this introspective spiritual discipline, making space in our days and nights for the regenerative power of the Spirit to renew our hearts and minds, the tempo of our souls begins to match that of Jesus. Our heart, the seat of our motivations, begins to beat in sync with Christ's. His peace becomes our peace. His joy becomes our joy. His love becomes our love.

As this happens, we are able to approach hot-button issues and contentious environments with the ability to regulate our emotions. We are able to contradict anxiety and outrage in a manner that is full of peace. This aroma of Christlikeness is what this world yearns for.

Sexual orientation and gender identity are deeply personal, deeply vulnerable aspects of the self. Every Christian who wrestles with these issues must discover what it looks like for Jesus to be Lord of our desires and our bodies. This is already a difficult, costly, emotional task. If churches and Christians can cultivate environments of deep peace and love, this task becomes livable, joyful, and healing. If we continue to spread anxiety like the flu, the task feels practically impossible. We are still the physical embodiment of Christ on the earth. We are still animated by the Holy Spirit: "He who raised Christ from the dead will also give life to your mortal bodies because of his Spirit who lives in you" (Romans 8:11).

REFLECTION QUESTIONS

1. What are some practical ways you and your church can live out the fruits of repentance?
2. What fears or assumptions keep us from being peacemakers in conversations about sexual orientation and gender identity? How can we bring those into prayer using the examen?
3. Where have you seen peacemaking lead to healing or reconciliation in this area? What can we learn from those moments?

9

CAN I GET A WITNESS?

To bear witness is to make our lives the stage on which the resurrected Christ appears.

Willie James Jennings

While reading about the most influential pastor in American history, I was caught off-guard by his generosity of spirit. In an undertold episode in Billy Graham's tremendous life, we see Graham urging a president toward compassion regarding a gay-sex scandal in his administration.

President Lyndon B. Johnson's top political adviser was a man named Walter Jenkins. In 1964, just under a year into Johnson's presidency, a story broke in the news that Jenkins had been busted not once but twice for having sex with a man. At this time homosexuality was both a crime and considered a mental illness. This would only mean scandal.

Johnson, coming into the presidency under stressful circumstances already in the wake of the Kennedy assassination, agonized over what this would do to the polls. It was here that Graham stepped in. On a telephone call with the president, he said, "You know, when Jesus dealt with people who had moral problems, like dear Walter had . . . he always dealt tenderly. Always. This is the way he handled it. Always. And that's the way I feel about it. I know the weaknesses of men, and the Bible says we're all sinners. . . . I just hope if you have any contact with him, you'll give him my love and understanding."[1]

In a political environment where President Johnson certainly would have been pressured to deal harshly and swiftly with his gay adviser, and where doing so would have brought kudos from his religious supporters, Graham gave counterintuitive advice. Not because he was secretly a progressive Christian with a revisionist approach to biblical sexual ethics but because he sought to be like Jesus. In this circumstance that meant dealing tenderly with a broken person. Not punishing him, not turning him into an ideological enemy, and not throwing him away, but treating him like a human being made in the image of God and someone Christ died for.

Graham is far from the only prominent evangelical who has modeled a posture toward our LGBTQ+ neighbors that invites us to move beyond anxious culture-warring. From C. S. Lewis, Francis Schaeffer, and John Stott in decades past to Alistair Begg and Timothy Keller more recently, many prominent followers of Jesus have blazed a better path forward when it comes to loving LGBTQ+ people. When it comes to peacemaking, bearing witness, and discipleship with our LGBTQ+ neighbors, history has much to teach us.

There has never been a golden age for the church. There has been no time in history when Christians perfectly reflected Christ to their culture, when there was no scandal, no compromise, no infighting. There is a temptation to whitewash the early church, as if they came out of the gate perfectly reflecting the way of Jesus. You need only to read Paul's letters in the New Testament to see this is not true.

Similarly, there has never been a time in history when every Christian was culpable in the errors of the church. Just as there has always been compromise in church history, there has also always been a faithful remnant modeling Jesus in beautiful and compelling ways. True witnesses have been present in every season of the church.

TAKING THE STAND AS A WITNESS

The word *witness* is key to a Christian sense of self, but we often misunderstand its meaning or ignore it all together. Consider Jesus' parting words to his followers in Acts 1:8. Right before he ascends, he charges his disciples with the following words: "But you will receive power when the Holy Spirit comes on you; and you will be my witnesses in Jerusalem, and in all Judea and Samaria, and to the ends of the earth."

The Greek word for "witness" in this brief teaching from Jesus is *martys*. If that looks to you like the word *martyr*, you're not mistaken. Like many Greek words, *martys* is layered with meaning. While translated as "witness" here, part of bearing witness is to live and proclaim the truth even if it leads to death.

This means there are no limits to the extent Christians will go to bear witness, even to the extent of losing their reputations, jobs, and very lives. This adds some much-needed gravitas to Jesus' instructions to his followers. Bearing witness to Jesus is not for the faint of heart. But, then again, neither is being a Christian.

This assignment from Jesus is not a suggestion or a guideline but a command that ought to be taken as seriously as our very lives.

But let's look at another meaning of what Jesus means by "witness." *Martys* was also a legal word in the ancient world. It served the same purpose then as our word *witness* does when somebody takes the stand in a court of law and testifies to something they have seen. We can safely assume from Jesus' words here that the world is like a cosmic courtroom and Christ is appealing to the court through his followers, who are on the stand as witnesses testifying to what they have discovered in him.

This beautiful truth is key to missional theology. Our primary task for evangelism, our key methodology, is to simply live lives and speak words that bear witness to Jesus. Not to make a sales pitch, not to literally "scare the hell out of people," not to coerce or manipulate them. But to live in a way that provokes curiosity. To live in such a way that our lives, words, and stories testify to world-redeeming beauty. Bearing witness is simply telling the truth about our union with Jesus, even in situations where we might feel tempted to suppress that part of ourselves.

In his book *Surrender to Love*, David Benner recounts coming to a confession of faith as a young child in response to a terrifying gospel presentation. He writes, "I was told that salvation was a gift of love, but it seemed strange to ask me to accept the gift at gunpoint."[2] If we bear witness to what we have seen in Jesus, we won't scare, shout, or manipulate people into the kingdom of God. Our assignment from Jesus is both simple and exceedingly difficult. We are to take what we have encountered of Jesus in the Scriptures, through his Spirit's work in our hearts, and in how he has changed our stories, and we are to embody that in our day-to-day lives. When we do this, we take the stand as credible witnesses in the world's court, where the case is to discover truth and goodness.

And yet many Christians act as if Acts 1:8 reads, "You will receive power when my Spirit comes on you, and you will be my prosecutors to the ends of the earth" or "you will be my defense attorneys to the ends of the earth." Rather than living lives and saying words that bear witness to the goodness, truth, and beauty of Jesus, many of us have come at LGBTQ+ people with a prosecutor's zeal, out to prove them guilty and see judgment pronounced. Or we have seen ourselves as defense attorneys, less combative, perhaps, but still falling short of Jesus' command. Whether it was to sound the alarm about marriage equality or drag queens reading books to kids in public libraries, we have sought to defend our case before the world's court, often with anxious outrage or hate-filled tirades.

Again, these are truths worth contending for. There is a way to bear witness to the truth without compromising our peacemaking vocation. Fear robs us of this.

Throughout history, when Christian communities have resolved to bear witness to what they have seen in Jesus, they found surprising ways to be a blessing to their culture and care for those society has harmed. As we learn to love our LGBTQ+ neighbors, we can gain substantial insight and guidance by looking backward.

AN ANCIENT WITNESS

At its conception in the ancient world, Christianity quickly became a dangerous movement to join. It was viewed with increasing hostility by the Roman Empire as it proved to be a legitimate philosophical and political threat to the Roman way of life. To join the church was to risk imprisonment, torture, and death. And yet, in spite of the cost of discipleship, the early church grew steadily and rapidly. How was that possible? Well, the church fought dark powers and principalities with the tactics of Jesus: radical inclusion, peacemaking, self-sacrificial love, and hospitality.

In his book *Water from a Deep Well*, theologian and historian Gerald Sittser shines light on the reputation of the early church among people outside the church. It was a reputation that looked markedly different from the American evangelical church's reputation with unchurched people today. Individuals did not become Christians in the ancient world without considerable risk to themselves and their loved ones, but the early church's fragrance was so irresistible that they deemed joining it worth the cost.

Sittser presents four characteristics the early church was known for among pagans in the ancient world. In other words, this was how non-Christian, Greek-god-worshiping pagans perceived the first Christians. As we consider these four qualities, let's also reflect on how contemporary churches could practice them today, and how doing so could help us remove the barriers that harm our LGBTQ+ neighbors. I have adapted some of Sittser's language to help us see how these attributes pertain to our moment.

They were an inclusive community in an exclusive world. Christianity began to develop a reputation for radical inclusion right from the start. Christians served, honored, and sacrificed for the types of people Roman elites wouldn't be caught dead in a room with. In a world that coveted exclusivity, the first Christians were motivated by the God-man who instructed them to care for "the least of these" (Matthew 25:40).

Pliny the Younger was a well-known thinker in ancient Rome and early critic of Christianity. He often observed that Christians seemed to include everyone, making no distinction in rank, appearance, wealth, education, age, or sex. This was scandalous in a society built on distinctions between rich and poor, in-their-prime and too old or too young, men and women. By this, Pliny argued that Christians were dishonorable, foolish, and stupid. To Pliny, it was no wonder so many slaves, women, and children, the most "appalling" in ancient society, were drawn to the Christian community.[3]

In a culture that prized power, wealth, authority, and a level of elitism that makes today's Ivy League professors look like *Beavis and Butt-Head*, the radical inclusivity of the early church revealed to the world what their God was like. He was the God who chastised the greedy, rebuked the powerful, ate meals with the dirty and left out, and invited tax collectors and sex workers to join his movement. This vision of radical inclusivity in the person of Jesus empowered the church to practice that same radical inclusion. And this inclusion became the church's dominant reputation in the ancient world.

What does radical inclusion look like in the church for our LGBTQ+ neighbors today? Some might say that true inclusion necessitates affirmation of same-sex marriage and all professed gender identities. Some argue that without affirmation we can't practice inclusion at all. For them, if churches do not revise their theology on sex, marriage, and gender, those churches will always be exclusive.

However, our world tends to conflate affirmation and inclusion, and this is unwise. First, those two different words have two different meanings. To affirm something is to declare that thing as true. Inclusion is the act of inviting someone in a group or structure. Today many people on both the theological left and theological right cannot imagine including someone without affirming them. However, to include only what you can affirm is to create a community of uniformity where everyone looks and acts the same. This is opposed to the New Testament vision of diverse community, where all types of people from all types of backgrounds come together as Christ's body.

In the imagination of Jesus, it was in fact possible to practice inclusion without affirmation. Look at Matthew 9:10: "While Jesus was having dinner at Matthew's house, many tax collectors and sinners came and ate with him and his disciples." Notice it does not say many former tax collectors and sinners. The guest list at Jesus' table included people who were still very much in the shameful profession of tax collecting and the fallen condition of sin. Jesus did not ask them to clean themselves up before they shared a meal with him. Repentance was not a prerequisite to table fellowship with the Son of God.

It's hard to overstate how disruptive Jesus was being here. In the ancient world, sharing a meal with somebody was not a neutral act. Whereas today I might be willing to grab lunch with somebody I've never met before, ancient adherents to Judaism were not so flippant. Gathering around a table in ancient Mediterranean culture was a sign of family, unity, and oneness. Jesus sharing a meal with tax collectors and sinners is about as punk rock and subversive as you can get. This is inclusion. This is Jesus saying, "No matter where you come from, or what you have done, or what you might do, you belong with me."

However, we do not see Jesus affirm anything that falls short of the divine ideal. There is no invitation from Jesus to the tax collectors and sinners that says, "You do you" or "Live your truth." Remember, Jesus' first sermon is one of repentance. And even a cursory reading of the teachings of Jesus shows he has a higher standard for consecrated sexuality than any other writer in Scripture. It is true that in many ways Jesus loosens the rigidity of his contemporaries' application of the Old Testament. But regarding sexuality, Jesus doesn't loosen the boundaries; he tightens them up. Just looking at somebody with lustful intent is on par with adultery. When it comes to sexuality, Jesus is anything but lenient.

Jesus sitting at the table with tax collectors and sinners reveals his method of discipleship: a broad door to a narrow way. It is the revelation that we are perfectly loved exactly as we are. It is also the invitation to leave behind our broken way of life in order to take on his beautiful way of life. Jesus practices radical inclusion and the call to belonging without affirming things beneath God's dream for humanity.

The church today would do well to follow the example of Jesus and the early Christians. In our places of worship, we are not in charge of the guest list; Jesus is. It's his church, not ours. As John the Baptist says, "The bride belongs to the bridegroom" (John 3:29). We're all guests at his table, and he invites anyone and everyone to sit with him, no matter how messy their stories.

That is radical inclusion. That is what our LGBTQ+ neighbors are aching for. LGBTQ+ people aren't ignorant. They know most churches do not affirm gay marriage or embrace trans identities.

If they are coming to church, it's very likely they are looking for something more than affirmation. They are looking for a meal with the God of the universe.

Let's take this a step further. What does inclusion look like for the thousands of LGBTQ+ people currently in our churches? Is it telling them they're welcome to sit in our chairs and give us money—but that's it? This is a pitiful discipleship strategy for anyone. Inclusion in church always welcomes and embraces. Eugene Peterson writes:

> Congregation is composed of people, who, upon entering a church, leave behind what people on the street name or call them. A church can never be reduced to a place where goods and services are exchanged. It must never be a place where a person is labeled. It can never be a place where gossip is perpetuated. Before anything else, it is a place where a person is named and greeted, whether implicitly or explicitly, in Jesus' name. A place where dignity is conferred.[4]

Dignifying our LGBTQ+ neighbors when they come to church looks like sitting with them, engaging them, expressing gratitude that they've visited. It's being aware that they likely had to muster a great deal of courage to come. It's inviting them to contribute their gifts. Maybe they have a knack for hospitality and making people feel welcome. Maybe they love technology, computers, sound systems, or lightboards. Maybe they like serving coffee, offering a warm welcome, helping set things up and tear things down, or playing an instrument. It's possible to include LGBTQ+ people in the life of the church without affirming behavior that goes against the traditional sexual ethic.

And if the LGBTQ+ person in question is in alignment with your church's stance on sexuality, gender, and marriage, it's time to shatter the glass ceiling and remove any manmade barrier that would keep them from serving in a church office. Remember, fallenness is different from sinfulness. Fallenness is a ramification of the chaos unleashed when Adam and Eve ate the fruit; sinfulness is a contribution to that chaos. My same-sex attraction, or another person's blindness, may be a result of the fall, but it is not sin in and of itself. When a person, any person, demonstrates proven spiritual maturity, theological alignment, and an aptitude for leadership, a just church will nurture those qualities rather than reject them.

Inclusion looks like inviting the LGBTQ+ person into your home, to your table, to know your family and community. It looks like bearing burdens and sharing dreams. It looks like calling out the best in them and mining their God-given potential. It looks like praying and laughing and weeping and eating and worshiping together. We can do all of this and more without revising what Scripture and the church have historically taught about sex, marriage, and gender.

The early church brought stability to an unstable world. Disease, crime, and war were everyday realities in the Roman Empire. Caesar's fear of losing power to competitive nations filled the empire with anxiety and outrage. And in just three hundred years, Antioch alone was hit by more than forty natural disasters that caused countless deaths.[5] In the midst of it all, the fledgling Christian community refused to have its peace robbed by external circumstances and rose to the occasion of loving their neighbors.

While anxiety, chaos, and pain swirled in the surrounding culture, early Christians stood apart—rooted in God's love and devoted to their neighbors. What truly distinguished them was their vision: The kingdom of God had broken into history through Jesus, and not even Rome could undo it. "Our citizenship is in heaven," Paul writes in Philippians 3:20.

These believers were not Caesar's tools but Christ's ambassadors. They did not live for security or power but for faithfulness, trusting that "perfect love casts out fear" (1 John 4:18 NRSVUE). Their confidence in God and commitment to love created a community that brought social and emotional stability to a culture in crisis. They were able to rise above disease, famine, war, and persecution because they followed a different King than the anxious Caesar.

They were the peacemakers Christ calls his followers to be. And Jesus' use of "peace" in this teaching from Matthew 5:9 would have invoked the Hebrew paradigm of shalom. Shalom isn't simply the absence of conflict; it is wholeness, the way things were always meant to be. So we could read Jesus as saying, "Blessed are the wholeness-makers."

From the first Christians under the threat of the Roman Empire to Saint Francis and his "little brothers and sisters" in the shadow of mass church corruption in the 1200s, from Dietrich Bonhoeffer and his fellow seminarians resisting German fascism in World War II to Dr. Martin Luther King Jr. and his nonviolent, enemy-loving movement in the face of racism and segregation, the muscularity of the church has always been found in its peacemaking capacity.

When our LGBTQ+ neighbors come to church, it's not uncommon for them to find emotional frailty instead of stability. We can be so concerned with winning a culture war that we forget the mission of God. This robs us of our peacemaking instincts and imparts an emotional brittleness that leads to emotional frailty. Not only that, but this frailty is often either directly pointed at LGBTQ+ people or manifested at great cost to them. Repeatedly Christians justify this frailty and anxiety by claiming to simply be telling the truth. However, if truth-telling comes at the expense of the fruit of the Spirit (in this case, the fruit of peace), it's likely we don't have a firm grasp on the truth as God sees it.

When Jesus tells us the truth, he does so without compromising love, joy, peace, patience, kindness, goodness, gentleness, faithfulness, and self-control.

Our current historic moment is marked by profound instability. If we were to survey the mental health of the secular population in America, we would see the words *anxiety* and *depression* come up again and again.[6] We have been living in what can only be described as a mental health crisis for some time now. LGBTQ+ people are among the most susceptible to this crisis.[7] We are also in a crisis of political polarization, a crisis of identity, and a crisis of conscience. American culture has not felt this unstable in my lifetime. It seems like every day we realize anew that secularism does not have the resources to guide us into a meaningful, flourishing life.

The early church offered a haven of stability in an unstable world. We can do this again. Imagine if our LGBTQ+ neighbors came into our church spaces and were surprised to find their anxieties calmed and their fears quieted. Imagine them coming into church bracing themselves for judgment, phobia, and debate and instead finding emotional and spiritual stability.

Now imagine that, over the next few decades, enough churches return to their peacemaking vocation that the reputation of the church is restored. Imagine that LGBTQ+ people feel no fear of phobia or judgment when they come to church. Does it sound too good to be true? It's not. It's possible. But it starts with us, and it starts today.

The early church loved until it hurt. In AD 165, and then again in AD 250, plagues swept over Rome. Scholars have a hard time calculating the exact number of deaths, but they estimate that these two plagues killed nearly half the population of Rome. Half the people in the most powerful empire on earth gone in less than a hundred years. Thousands of people dying every day.

In the wealthy cities people were dying too fast to be cremated ceremonially, as was the Roman custom, so the dead were taken to impoverished parts of the empire and left on roads, in fields, and in front of houses. These decaying, plague-ridden bodies spread disease to the poor and caused them to die at astronomically higher rates than the rich. The Roman Empire fell into a deep despair.[8]

The plagues struck everyone, pagan and Christian alike. But Christians responded differently. They didn't abandon the sick, call the disease God's punishment, or despair. They trusted Christ's comfort, clung to hope in the resurrection, and believed God's love would prevail. This faith propelled them into unprecedented acts of service. Dionysius of Alexandria writes:

> Most of our brother Christians showed unbounded love and loyalty, never sparing themselves and thinking only of one another. Heedless of danger, they took charge of the sick, attending to their every need and ministering to them in Christ. . . . Many, in nursing and curing others, transferred their death to themselves and died in their stead.[9]

Christians began collecting dead bodies, at great risk to themselves, and burying them on their own property. They began opening their homes to become hospitals for the sick to die in while being cared for, to die with dignity. They fed and housed those whose livelihood was impacted by the plague. While it was not uncommon for Romans to enslave the children of those who had died from the plague—or abandon them to the streets if they were deemed to be of no use—the Christians housed them, fed them, raised them, and taught them trade skills.

In the ancient world, humans' primary relationship to the gods was one of appeasement. And the gods could be appeased only via a proper sacrifice or offering. The Christian God was different. This God loved all of humanity, and this God could be appeased only by his worshipers also loving all of humanity.

This self-sacrificial love is a cornerstone of what it means to follow Jesus, as he demonstrated during his life and ministry. Near the end of Jesus' teaching in Matthew 11, he addresses criticisms thrown at him by the religious elite of his day: "For John came neither eating nor drinking, and they say, 'He has a demon.' The Son of Man came eating and drinking, and they say, 'Here is a glutton and a drunkard, a friend of tax collectors and sinners.' But wisdom is proved right by her deeds" (Matthew 11:18-19).

Jesus made the conscious choice to share bread and wine with the most disreputable in society. He practiced table fellowship with the dirty and left out. In the church I planted, we talked a lot about how the cross is the definitive example of Jesus' love, and it is. But this can sometimes eclipse the other examples of self-sacrifice we see in Jesus before the cross. It is no small thing to sacrifice respect, trust, and your own reputation with the most influential people in the place you live. That takes tremendous courage, conviction, and love.

The self-sacrificial love of Jesus will often look like compromise to people who love religious observance more than people. But we know Jesus cannot compromise God's standards. What will it look like for us to self-sacrificially love our LGBTQ+ neighbors?

Instead of being fearful or angry about our local Pride parade, let's find creative ways to bring Christ's kindness to that context. Instead of offering a corrective Bible verse to a loved one when they come out to us, let's offer a hug, like my best friend did for me when I came out him. Instead of posting on social media anxiety-filled toxins about drag queens in libraries, let's learn the stories of the LGBTQ+ people around us, because they are worth knowing. Instead of using the weapons of this world to wage a war, let's use the weapon of the kingdom of God, the weapon of love. After all, as followers of Jesus, we are called to love our enemies. And when we love our enemies, we find we no longer have enemies, only neighbors.

The early church valued and cared for all of human life, from womb to tomb. In the Roman Empire, people were only as valuable as their contribution. Slavery was as common to the Romans as electricity is to us. It was a deeply pragmatic society. So unwanted children, people who experienced divergent mental or physical needs, and slaves were often subjected to horrendous, violent, and sometimes lethal treatment.

The early church, however, operated under the assumption that Christ died for all and so loved all. It wasn't a very pragmatic way to live in the short run, but it was a Christlike way to live. And in the long run it proved to be so pragmatic that, today, we have non-Christian people and institutions dedicated to Christian innovations. Christians started the first hospitals, orphanages, eldercare homes, homeless shelters, and food shelters. No one was beneath them. No one was valued by what they could contribute but by the fact that Christ loved and died for them.[10]

The church took to heart Paul's words to the church in Ephesus: "For we are God's handiwork, created in Christ Jesus to do good works, which God prepared in advance for us to do" (Ephesians 2:10). This word translated as "handiwork" is the Greek word *poema*. We derive our word "poem" from *poema*. Other translations say "masterpiece" or "workmanship." A *poema* is a work of art.

My wife is a gifted painter. When we were dating she painted what has become my most prized possession. Knowing my favorite band is Switchfoot, she created a large canvas constellation of all Switchfoot's album art up to that point. It is stunning, and virtually everyone we show it to assumes we bought it from Switchfoot's merch shop. We even got the band members to sign it, and they were blown away. My wife has painted a lot of lovely things over the years, many of which hang in our house. But this Switchfoot painting is her masterpiece, it's her *poema*. It's the first thing I'll grab if our house is on fire.

That is how God sees us. We are his works of art. That is who we are, and that is how we are to treat one another. We are called to practice self-sacrificial love not in spite of people's worth but because of it. Every human being is made in the image of God and therefore of immeasurable value. How we treat our neighbors, including our LGBTQ+ neighbors, should reflect this profound theological certainty.

To be a Christian is to see the value inherent in all of humanity, and the deepest forms of theological compromise stem from a failure to do so. Before we quote a verse or communicate a theological stance to our LGBTQ+ neighbors, we should stop and ask: Do they know they are loved, made with divine purpose, and of inestimable value? Are they convinced of it? If not, that is our starting place, not correction.

When we are dealing with culturally combative topics, it's easy to become motivated by victory instead of love. We want to win the argument, not the person. If we were trying to get our LGBTQ+ neighbors inside and outside the church merely to comply with a historical sexual ethic, then sure, coercion might be a good tactic. But that is not our goal. Surrender to Jesus is the lifelong goal of every Christian, and it is ultimately what we invite people into as they consider union with Christ.

We want our LGTBQ+ neighbors and everyone else to surrender not to our political leader of choice, to governmental policies, or to approved school library books. We want them to surrender to Jesus and his love. And intentional, Jesus-like love is the only way to get them there.

WITNESSING GROWTH

The early church grew because of its witness. Its members established an inclusive, stable community in an exclusive, unstable world. They showed self-sacrificial love to all humans in a society that valued power, dominance, and perfection. The early church lived counterculturally and embraced all the social and physical risk that accompanied their witness. As a result, the Christian witness reshaped the moral imagination of the world as we know it.

Research has shown that 86 percent of LGBTQ+ people were raised in religious homes and 54 percent left the church after turning eighteen, with more leaving later on in life.[11] If the church had broadly clung to its values of radical inclusion, cultural stability, self-sacrificial love, and value for all of life, it's likely that many of our LGBTQ+ neighbors would not have felt the need to leave. It's a sobering but necessary idea to wrestle with. And there is cause for hope. In truth, we have everything we need to embody the witness of our ancestors and mothers.

REFLECTION QUESTIONS

1. Which of the early church's values do you think the modern church struggles with most—and why?
2. What does it mean to truly value a person's life "from womb to tomb"?
3. What would it take for LGBTQ+ people to feel like they truly belonged in your church or family?

10

WHEN SOMEONE YOU LOVE COMES OUT

No one reaches out to you for compassion and empathy so you can teach them how to behave better. They reach out because they believe in our capacity to know our darkness well enough to sit in the dark with them.

Brené Brown

I was sitting in the booth of a shabby diner waiting for my dad to arrive. My palms were sweaty, chest tight with anxiety, and jaw clenched. Worst case scenario? This would be my last conversation with my dad. Best case scenario? My anxiety was so high I couldn't imagine one.

I had just been fired from the church my family had attended for over a decade, one I'd spent five years with on staff. I was fired because my experience of same-sex attraction had come to light, and my pastor deemed it best for me, my wife, and the youth I ministered to that I step down. I had spent several days avoiding my dad's phone calls as I tried to find a way to tell him I'd been fired without telling him why.

My dad was a hardworking blue-collar man who'd spent childhood summers on a farm in Idaho. He never gave me a reason to suspect he would withhold his love from me, but he also raised us to be deep-red conservatives, and we rarely spoke about LGBTQ+ issues in our home.

But I could not come up with a compelling lie. No, in this situation, only the truth would do. So I called him and invited him to this unexceptional diner to tell him a secret twelve years in the making.

My dad arrived and sat down in the booth, and we made small talk long enough to order our food and have it arrive. It was painfully awkward, as my dad and I are both quite bad at the whole small talk thing. As soon as the waitress set our food down and walked away, I began to spill my guts.

"Dad . . . I have to tell you something. And I don't know how to say it so I'm just gonna say it. And it's probably going to be really hard for you to hear. I was asked to step down from the church this week. I was asked to step down because, well, since I was about eleven I have been attracted to guys.

"I don't know if I'm bisexual or gay, but I know I have wrestled with this for most of my life. I hate it. I don't want it. I would give anything not to be this way. It's why I was so depressed as a kid. I love Jesus and I love my wife, and I am not giving either of those things up. I never will. But I'm not straight, Dad. I'm so sorry."

My dad, obviously shocked, just stared at me for a moment. Our food was getting cold. Neither of us cared. He looked down at his food—out of shame, I thought. But then he took he glasses off and looked up at me. His eyes were filled with tears. To this day I can count on one hand the number of times I have seen my dad cry. Then he said something I did not expect.

"Tony, I'm sorry," he said. "I'm sorry you didn't grow up in a home where it was safe for you to say this to me sooner. But I love you. And you're still my son."

Now I was looking down at the table. As usual, my feeble attempts at predicting the future had failed me. I did not account for the possibility that he would respond with love and an apology. I wanted to cry, but I refrained. As I'm sure you're picking up by now, Scarcello men are not great at showing our emotions.

This is probably my favorite moment between my dad and me. It's a story that makes me proud to be his son, and I love telling it. It is the first thing that comes to mind when I am asked, as I frequently am, what the best way to respond is when someone you love comes out to you.

I love it when people ask this question. Not only because it reminds me of my dad and me at that second-rate diner, but because it shows that the person inquiring cares about handling that conversation well. And we should care. The first thing someone hears when they come out to a loved one sets the tone in that relationship for a while.

A bad reaction to the news that someone is not heterosexual or cisgender is devastating, but a loving reaction is redemptive. Still, when a loved one comes out to us it can be a shock, and we don't always know the right thing to say or do. So here are just a few tips.

AFFIRM YOUR LOVE FOR THEM

This becomes more important the closer you are to the person. Often the loved one coming out is fearful that divulging this information will lead to losing your love. That fear is devastating. No matter your beliefs on gender identity or same-sex attraction, it is paramount that the first things you say are words of love and affirmation of their value.

In his book *The Soul of Shame*, Dr. Curt Thompson notes that we are born "looking for someone looking at us," and we remain in this searching mode our whole lives.[1] When your loved one comes out to you, that is a moment to let them know they are seen and loved by you. It is an opportunity to quell the lie that says they must hide to be loved.

Losing my role as a youth pastor, for the reasons I lost it, led to me being looked at and talked about differently by some. It was almost as if people finding out this secret reshaped their view of me. I wasn't "me" to them anymore. I was something else, something less safe than they'd thought. When my dad said to me, "You're still my son," it contradicted the shaming voices in my head that had me convinced I was about to be disowned.

When people share the tender, vulnerable parts of their stories with a loved one and are received with open arms, shame withers and wounds begin to heal. My dad saying, "You're still my son" was him saying, in a sense, "You are not a monster. I don't see you differently. I won't treat you differently. You still belong to me."

When a loved one comes out, tell them you love them and this news does not alter their standing with you. They need to hear this. When we do this we build trust. They will continue to invite you in, and you will continue to foster intimacy with them.

IF YOU NEED TIME TO PROCESS, TAKE IT

Sometimes people come out to us and it catches us off guard. Especially for parents, this moment can lead to grief and feelings of failure. It can also lead to feelings of profound fear. Fear for the loved one, fear for the choices they will make, fear for how they will be treated, fear that people will blame the parent for the child's orientation.

While it's normal to experience these emotions, it's important not to make your loved one carry the weight of your fear and grief. As one mentor has said to me, "When fear is running the show, love is repressed." We cannot love well and be fearful. Love is focused on the other; fear is often fixated on the self.

It's also normal to grieve, especially if your child is the one coming out to you. You may have had dreams of your kids marrying and giving you grandkids. Your loved one may be leaving the faith, which is also cause for profound sadness. Just try not to make your grief their grief. Don't put them in a situation where they have to manage your emotions for you. Doing so will likely result in you saying things you'll regret and building a wall between you and them.

If your loved one is coming out as trans, and they wish to be identified by a different name or gender, that can also feel like a devastating blow. When your daughter, whose name you prayed for and felt led by God to give her, no longer wants to be called by that name or referred to as your daughter, that is heavy stuff. You are going to grieve that. It's going to feel personal. Remember that it is not personal. In fact, what your loved one is experiencing is not about you at all. We're all doing the best we can with the tools we have.

So if you need a minute to process the news before you say too much, it is better to take it than to say something you can't take back. It is okay to say, "I did not expect this, and I don't know what to say. I don't want to say the wrong thing and hurt you. Is it okay if I take some time to process and revisit it with you? Know that I love you and we will definitely talk more."

If you need to do this, make sure to be specific about how much time you need. If you need an hour or a day, let them know. Then, be intentional to name your feelings with trusted confidants and with the Lord. Seek wisdom, and return to the conversation in love. You may have to do this more than once, and that is okay. Just don't let too much time pass before you revisit the conversation.

I would strongly encourage you to find a few safe friends who love Jesus to talk to and grieve with as needed. This experience can feel isolating and devastating. You will be tempted to put that grief on your loved one. But it's not theirs to bear. Not yet. There may be a time down the road to discuss how this all makes you feel, but not now. They are dealing with their own fears and confusion. You are free to deal with yours. Remember, space to process is not the same as terminating the relationship or even a sign of decreased intimacy. It is a way to show kindness to yourself and the other person.

REMIND THEM JESUS STILL LOVES THEM

There is a fair chance that your loved one assumes God is giving up on them, is mad at them, or has rejected them. They may be convinced that if they're honest about their experience of same-sex attraction or gender dysphoria then they cannot be in loving union with God too. I cannot stress enough how important it is to remind them of their divine belovedness. Remind them they are still God's image bearers, made with intention and of immeasurable value. Remind them that, as the famous Psalm 23 concludes, his goodness and mercy will follow them all the days of their life.

They may make choices that contradict the historic teaching of Scripture or go against the grain of God's ideal. They may embrace a theology that is entirely different from yours. They may ask uncomfortable questions and express doubt that God even exists. Wherever they're at, whatever untruth they might believe, the truth that they are beloved of the Lord will never change. And if you want them to be convinced of anything, you want them to be convinced of that.

ASK FOR GRACE

It is quite an adjustment to learn that someone you love and thought was straight or cisgender is not, especially if that loved one is requesting you use a different name and different pronouns. You are likely going to accidentally say something clumsy or downright offensive. It's a good idea, from the get-go, to say something along the lines of, "I am committed to loving you well in this, but I don't always know what the right thing to say is." Or, if you agree to use their chosen name, "I'm used to calling you X, and it's going to take some time to remember to call you Y."

PICK THE RIGHT FIGHTS

On that note, you may have complicated feelings about referring to your loved one by their chosen name and pronouns. Or if your loved one is gay, you may not know what to do if they decide to date or even marry someone of the same sex. Do you welcome their partner into the family? Attend their wedding? Confront them and establish distance until they are willing to repent?

These are real questions that require nuancing. For some people, it can feel disingenuous, dishonest, or enabling to use a person's chosen names and pronouns or attend a same-sex wedding. I don't want to dismiss this choice, as I believe the genuine concern here for most people is a commitment to what is true and right.

One should take these questions to prayer and wise counsel, and the motivation must always be love. If you find yourself having to confront these questions, I suggest that these might not be the right fights to pick. If your loved one is at the point of dating the same sex or changing their name, then being confrontational can feel like policing language and behavior. It can feel like you have taken it upon yourself to be their sin manager, even if you don't mean to. We are not called to be each other's sin managers but to be witnesses to the love and truth of Jesus, as well as his kindness that leads to repentance.

The love and truth of Jesus, that is our fight. Ask yourself, what is going to best communicate that love and truth to them? What is going to help them personally experience it? What is going to make them curious about the way of Jesus? My suggestion is to err on the side of grace and respect. It is gracious and respectful to honor boundaries our trans loved ones put in place regarding how they wish to be identified, even if we fundamentally disagree with these choices.

If you do feel like you must pick the pronoun or wedding fight, you need to recognize that these fights tend to create distance and misunderstanding in relationships, not intimacy and honesty. I have seen some people approach the conversation with high levels of intensity, often pressuring their LGBTQ+ loved one into coming to conclusions they don't actually hold. In an attempt to appease the desires of their loved ones, a queer person may abstain from embracing a trans identity or a same-sex romantic relationship. Not because they share theological convictions but because they are afraid of being rejected or disregarded. Sometimes, the queer loved one will cave under the weight of our anxiety and do as we say to appease us and protect the relationship.

Let me humbly pose this as food for thought, especially for parents and church leaders: As a Christ-loving parent or church leader, our goal should never be to make the people under our care feel the need to appease us or disingenuously cave to our demands out of fear that we will withdraw our love for them. That is not discipleship in the way of Jesus; that is coercion and manipulation. Oftentimes the high levels of intensity we bring to these conversations are fueled by a desire to control the outcome.

Again, when fear is running the show, love is repressed. When love is repressed, Christlikeness is forgone. We do not control the outcomes, even if we think we can. Attempts at seizing control, whether through manipulation, coercion, ultimatums, guilt trips, or growing cold in the relationship, these are signs we have stopped trusting God to be a good Father, stopped trusting Christ to be a gracious Redeemer, and stopped trusting the Holy Spirit to be a Wonderful Counselor.

Remember, only a non-anxious presence, only a peacemaker, can interrupt vicious cycles of anxiety.

DON'T MAKE ASSUMPTIONS

One of the questions that comes after "What do I say when they come out to me?" is, "What do I do after that initial conversation?" That's a fair and substantial question. After all, we have a whole life to live after that first talk. And I don't think we can go wrong in asking thoughtful, curious questions.

When a loved one comes out to us, it can be easy to jump to all sorts of assumptions about their intentions. Do they plan on dating people of the same sex? Are they committed to celibacy? Are they open to dating people of the opposite sex? Are they unsure? Are they gay, trans, both? Do they plan to change their name, get hormone therapy, ask to be addressed by different pronouns, or seek gender reassignment surgery? Or are they just inviting you in to knowing the turmoil they feel in their own body?

Assumptions are how we make sense of things we think we know but we don't actually know. So rather than making assumptions, ask, "What does this mean for you?" You may be surprised by the answer you get.

INVITE THEM TO CONSIDER THEIR GUIDE FOR MORAL WISDOM

It might be important to ask your loved one what they are consulting for moral wisdom. None of us come at morality in a vacuum. None of us decide the mechanics of reality on our own. People who define morality for themselves and use their own imaginations to define the nature of ultimate reality are rarely stable, wise, healthy people. We all look to some outside source to make sense of life and how to live it well.

So ask your loved one, "What are you looking to for moral guidance as you process this?" Get them thinking about it. Is it Scripture and the way of Jesus, or is it something else? A book? A social media influencer? TikTok? A documentary? A string of YouTube videos?

If the answer is something other than Scripture or the way of Jesus, ask them to examine the fruit of that thing they're consulting. What is the fruit of allowing social media or postmodernist philosophy to dictate our moral formation? What is the natural result of following our feelings and desires as our highest authority? And what is the fruit of a life lived out of continuity with the way of Jesus?

This is an important question for all of us to answer. The things we look to for moral wisdom determine the quality and the direction of our lives. And those who tether themselves to the way of Jesus report higher rates of peace, joy, and satisfaction than those who don't.[2] It's not that following Jesus leads to a pain-free life; it's that it leads to an abundant life. The fruit of the Spirit (love, joy, peace, patience, kindness, goodness, gentleness, faithfulness, and self-control) are the qualities of a life devoted to God.

ASK, "HOW CAN I SUPPORT YOU?"

It is also important to ask how you can support your loved one, and in ways that don't contradict orthodoxy. Do they want to do a theological deep dive, or do they need a loving presence to process with? Do they want this to be an ongoing discussion, or would they rather it be left alone until they bring it up again? Do they want your advice, or do they need a little space?

In other words, seek your loved one's consent before forcing your questions, answers, and solutions on them. If they are not open to your input, or if they flat-out don't want it, it will fall on deaf ears and damage the relationship. Of course, you cannot "support" a loved one's sin, and there are tough conversations that should be had, but allow your loved one the dignity of consenting to those conversations. Remember, kindness, grace, and love lead to repentance, but coercion, arguing, and manipulation are unrecognizable in God's kingdom.

HELP BROADEN THEIR VISION OF CHRISTIAN SINGLENESS

If you're like me, you grew up with a vision of Christianity that viewed marriage and children as necessities for life. It was assumed that all of us would get married and have kids. If we did, we "arrived" at some higher plane of maturity, while single people were often patronized to and treated as secondhand citizens in the kingdom of God.

Your church likely has marriage ministries, book clubs, and retreats to help strengthen the marital bonds of people in your church. All beautiful things. However, singleness as an honorable life path may be ignored all together. Churches that do have singles ministries often focus on how to be faithfully single until marriage (again, assuming that path is inevitable), and those ministries often become the church's de facto matchmaking program.

This way of thinking assumes things about followers of Jesus that the Bible does not assume. Obviously, marriage is an important, theologically rich paradigm that should be honored, revered, and taken seriously. But it is not the only paradigm for Christian living in the Bible. In fact, depending on what section you're reading of the New Testament, you might think Scripture discourages us from getting married at all. I mean, look at Paul's words in 1 Corinthians 7:8: "Now to the unmarried and widows I say: It is good for them to stay unmarried, as I do."

The deeply Freudian assumption that we are all ultimately driven by carnal sexual desires, and that to abstain from those desires for too long is inhuman, has infiltrated our culture and our churches. Whereas secularism's answer to this assumption is hookup culture, the church's answer is to teach that it's normative for everybody to get married. After all, how can we be expected to live a fulfilling life without sex?

This is problematic for a number of reasons. Chief among them is that we worship, follow, and are saved by a thirty-three-year-old virgin. Jesus managed to live a fully flourishing life without getting married, having sex, or having children. We also have the witness of Jesus' greatest interpreter, the apostle Paul. The man who has given us most of our theological paradigms never married and never had children.

If the sexual revolution has made an idol out of sexual pleasure and personal autonomy, the church made an idol of the American vision of the nuclear family. The truth? Not everybody is supposed to get married. Some people might actually be much happier if they never get married. And contrary to the ridiculous PR campaign propagated by a pornified culture, it is possible to live a fulfilling life without sex.

HELP BROADEN THEIR VISION OF SEXUALITY

As one celibate gay friend taught me, "I can live without sex, but I can't live without love." God does not promise that all of us will experience satisfying sex lives, or that all of us even will have a sex life at all. See Paul, John the Baptist, Mother Teresa, John Stott, Henri Nouwen, and Jesus for examples of this.

Erotic consummation is not promised. But intimacy is commanded. Jesus actually commands a type of love that is willing to go to the grave for the other, and the context for that command isn't marriage: "My command is this: Love each other as I have loved you. Greater love has no one than this: to lay down one's life for one's friends" (John 15:12-13). We are to love one another as Jesus has loved us. How has Jesus loved us? Generously, sacrificially, and intimately.

One of the key things ungodly Christian teaching on sexuality misses is that our sexual energies drive us to seek all types of intimacy, not just physical pleasure. Our word "sex" comes from the Latin word *sarx*, which means to sever. There's almost an understanding here that we have been severed from something or someone. Severed from God, from community, from who we were made to be.

Our sexuality is our most primal attempt to reattach the internal sense of severing and alienation we all feel. Our Catholic brothers and sisters call upon the ancient Greek word *eros* to describe this sensation. While at its most elementary *eros* is translated as "erotic," many leading Catholic thinkers, such as Pope John Paul II, Ronald Rolheiser, and Christopher West, argue that this is an overly reductionist translation. West writes:

> Eros, as St. John Paul II said, "implies the upward impulse of the human heart toward what is true, good and beautiful." When you watch a movie that grabs hold of you that's eros being awakened in your heart. . . . Eros is the desire

of the human heart for God—for Truth, for Goodness, for Beauty. It passes by way of finite things, but launches us to infinite things.[3]

If it is true that eros is "the upward impulse of the human heart toward what is true, good, and beautiful," then eros is the energy within that seeks to unsever that which has been severed. This "unsevering" can happen through intercourse in marriage, but not only through intercourse. Sexuality, or eros, seeks to undo the great severing and is the force that drives us out of isolation and into intimacy. Intimacy means baring our soul, standing emotionally naked before another. That is not erotic or perverted but a deeply Christian value.

If you have the ear of a loved one coming out to you, it would be wise to help them see that being celibate does not mean being alone and unloved. And being married or sexually active does not mean wholeness and nirvana. Invite them into your space. Spend birthdays, holidays, and vacations together. Be the church to them. This does not erase the grief of not getting married or having kids. But if a loved one in our church chooses celibacy, either because they are not straight or for any other reason, we have the responsibility to surround them with New Testament family. And their choice not to marry does not mean they lose an outlet for eros.

As Ronald Rolhesier, my Catholic Gandalf, writes, "It's not good to be alone, and sexuality (eros) is the fire within us that at every level of our being, conscious and unconscious, body and soul, drives us outward beyond our aloneness, toward family, community, friendship, companionship, procreation, co-creation, celebration, delight, and consummation."

PLAY THE LONG GAME OF LOVE

Remember there are no quick fixes to someone's same-sex attraction or gender dysphoria. In fact, in most cases, there is no "fix" at all. One error I have seen pastors, parents, and loved ones make time and again is rushing to find a solution to a person's same-sex attraction, gender dysphoria, or decision to date or transition.

This is totally understandable. The temptation is to find a way to make the scary, painful thing go away. To quickly find a way to get the person coming out to you to see your side of things and do as you want them to. However, there is no quick solution to a person's orientation. There are no quick ways to talk someone out of dating people of the same sex or identifying as trans. When someone comes out to you, you are entering into a long, slow journey.

Any attempts at shortcuts on this journey will likely result in losing trust and intimacy with the person coming out to you. Many people jump the gun when a loved one comes out. They throw Bible verses at the person; they send them articles and books about Christian sexuality; they encourage them to seek treatment or to pray for "healing" from their orientation.

Ultimately, these attempts are unfruitful if the person coming out is not asking for or wanting those things from you. When we do things like this, we lose influence in the life of the person coming out. We are no longer viewed as safe people to talk and process with. And if they cannot talk with you without feeling judged or being beat over the head with the Bible, they will find someone who won't do those things.

Friend, believe me when I tell you that, painful as it may be, you want to meet someone in their court. You want to be a safe and trusted source of wisdom for them. And sometimes that means biting your tongue and simply listening. You do not know what the future holds. Your loved one will, like all of us, handle this scenario imperfectly. They may make harmful decisions or reject Christ's vision for their body and sexuality for a while.

As scary as that is, it is also so important not to underestimate the work of the Spirit and the power of prayer. That can sound trite, but it is actually the most powerful thing you can offer. God loves your loved one more than you ever could. God knows the beginning and the end. The Spirit of God is at work in the world, drawing people to himself, speaking healing, reconciliation, and love. God will not let your loved one go. And there will be a moment, possibly years down the road, when your loved one needs input from a Bible-loving, Spirit-filled, prayerful follower of Jesus.

It's a long game, loving people. This is true of all people, not just kids and congregants who are queer. This long game can feel exhausting, sad, and scary. But patience is the nature of New Testament love. "Love is patient," the apostle Paul tells us in 1 Corinthians 13:4. More than a theological stance, more than a doctrinal statement, more than knowing all the right passages of Scripture, we are called upon to love patiently.

REMEMBER YOUR PRIMARY VOCATION IN CHRIST

Finally, I want to reflect on a key moment in the life of Jesus. In the Gospel of John, Jesus' biographer ends his account in a weighty way. John 20 tells a story of Jesus' disciples gathered together in a private room, and out of nowhere Jesus appears among them. I imagine this was extremely unsettling to the disciples. Then Jesus says, "Peace be with you," which is hilarious since he probably just scared the netherworld out of them. Then, starting in verse 20, the weighty thing happens:

> He showed them his hands and his side. Then the disciples rejoiced when they saw the Lord. Jesus said to them again, "Peace be with you. As the Father has sent me, so I send you." When he had said this, he breathed on them and said to them, "Receive the Holy Spirit." (John 20:20-22, NRSV).

There is one key observation I want to make in this passage. There is a statement here that might have alarmed the disciples just as much as Jesus magically appearing in the room with them: "As the Father has sent me, so I send you."

The disciples of Jesus are being sent out by Jesus just as Jesus was sent out by the Father.

That is daunting for anyone paying attention. How has the Father sent Jesus? Jesus was sent into this world in total union with the Father, empowered by the Spirit, with the mission of proclaiming and inaugurating the kingdom of heaven. In fact, in a different Gospel account, Luke reveals exactly how Jesus has been sent out.

In Luke 3:21-22, Jesus is baptized by his wild-eyed cousin when the Holy Spirit descends upon him in physical appearance like a dove. The Father's voice from heaven proclaims, "You are my Son, whom I love; with you I am well pleased."

Right after this, in Luke 4:1-14, Jesus fasts in the wilderness, where he is tempted by the father of lies. Jesus enters the wilderness "full of the Holy Spirit," does spiritual warfare with his adversary, then leaves the wilderness. But this time he's not merely full of the Spirit. This time he leaves "in the power of the Spirit."

Immediately after this Jesus announces his mission to his contemporaries in a synagogue. Some scholars say that in the ancient world, a rabbi began his ministry by selecting a passage from the Hebrew Bible (what we would call the Old Testament) to be a sort of thesis statement for his teaching career. He would publicly read this passage in the synagogue as a way to proclaim what his ministry would be about.[4] Jesus selected his passage from the scroll of Isaiah and publicly announced:

> "The Spirit of the Lord is on me,
> because he has anointed me
> to proclaim good news to the poor.
> He has sent me to proclaim freedom for the prisoners
> and recovery of sight for the blind,
> to set the oppressed free,
> to proclaim the year of the Lord's favor." (Luke 4:18-19)

Jesus' ministry thesis statement was that he would bring good news to the lowly, that he would bring liberation and revelation, that he would ease the bonds of oppression, and that his whole life would be a proclamation of God's love and kindness.

Back to John 20, where followers of Jesus are sent out by Jesus just as he was sent out by the Father. He was sent out assured of his belovedness, ready to battle forces of chaos and deceit, full of power from the Spirit, and living a life of proclamation of the love of God. We, as students in the way of Jesus, are to orient our lives around doing likewise.

I am under the strong conviction that, as Eugene Peterson wrote, "The Bible, all of it, is livable."[5] The call of God on humanity is not merely to assume the title "Christian" but to become practitioners in the way of Jesus. Just as the Twelve were chosen to do what Jesus did, so we too are chosen for such a task.

When we enter into the school of Jesus, a radical shift happens in how we understand ourselves. We are sent-out ones. We are harbingers of new creation and reconcilers of heaven and earth. We are no longer just a parent, friend, pastor, manager, coworker, son, daughter, sister, or brother. We are sent-out ones.

When your loved one comes out to you, no matter your relational touchpoint with them, you are a sent-out one. May your response be one that reflects the liberation-bringing, burden-lifting, truth-telling, Spirit-filled, and loving-champion Jesus.

REFLECTION QUESTIONS

1. What are some of the biggest challenges you would experience if a loved one unexpectedly came out to you?
2. What's at stake if we respond poorly to a loved one coming out?
3. What would you need to hear if you had to confess something very personal and scary?

11

A BIGGER TABLE

The saints are those who have experienced the love of God and have allowed that love to shape their lives. They teach us what it means to live in grace.

Richard Foster

Much of this book has been a survey of the church's past, both the beautiful and the ugly. I chose to do this because we are, at least partially, products of our past. When we look behind us we can see the failures and the successes of our ancestors and mothers.

It's true, many LGBTQ+ people have lived in ways that reject the heart of God. Many of them, like all of us, are tempted to choose autonomy from God and live by their own standards of right and wrong. But there are at least two queer people from recent church history who have shaped the church in more profound ways than we might realize.

I cannot think of a more appropriate way for us to conclude our time together than by reflecting on these two men and acknowledging how they have influenced the church for the better. Like John Wesley, Martin Luther King Jr., Mother Teresa, Justin the Martyr, Claire of Assisi, and Dietrich Bonhoeffer, imagining what the modern church would look like without the witness of these two men is a horrifying thought.

ANGUISHED DEPTH

Henri Nouwen (1932–1996) was a Dutch-born Catholic priest, theologian, and author who became widely known for his insights into faith, vulnerability, and the intersection of psychology and spirituality. A prolific writer, he penned more than forty books on the spiritual life, including *The Return of the Prodigal Son*, *The Wounded Healer*, and *In the Name of Jesus*. His work has influenced readers all over the world for decades now, including me. The many people touched by Henri Nouwen's work include Fred Rogers, Susan Sarandon, Martin Sheen, Bono, Oprah, and Brené Brown.

I first came across Nouwen's work right after I was let go from my role as youth pastor and storming over my faith, the church, and my identity. I was angry, doubtful, and deep in grief. His book *From Mourning to Dancing* was the first book I'd read that made me feel understood by the author. Understood in ways I never anticipated. Since then, I can safely say I am almost always reading or rereading one of Nouwen's books. There is not a day of my life that goes by that isn't governed, in some way, by Nouwen's writing.

An aspect of Nouwen's life that remained largely private during his lifetime was his struggle with sexual orientation. As a same-sex-attracted man who was also Catholic clergy, he lived with a profound internal tension, struggling to reconcile his deep longing for companionship with his commitment to his faith and priestly vows of celibacy. He was open with close friends about his struggle but chose not to share it widely, perhaps due to his fear of rejection within the church. His inner conflict became a "wound" that he carried with him, a source of suffering that influenced his understanding of God's love and grace.[1]

In his work, his anguish is clear. He writes openly about loneliness, suffering, and the need for authentic community, inviting others into a space where wounds can be transformed into sources of healing. In one of his most popular works, Nouwen writes, "Ministry can indeed be a witness to the living truth that the wound, which causes us to suffer now, will be revealed to us later as the place where God intimated his new creation."[2] Nouwen's openness to both joy and sorrow allowed him to connect deeply with others, especially those who felt marginalized or unseen.

Nouwen's legacy offers a powerful example for us as we seek to navigate the complex intersection of faith, sexuality, theological faithfulness, and inclusivity. Embracing our LGBTQ+ neighbors in the church is not about relinquishing a sexual ethic but living out the commandment to love one's neighbor as oneself. Nouwen's life reflects the conviction that it is possible to experience same-sex attraction and to contribute something vital to the church.

In a time when our loved ones suffer from anxiety and depression on nearly cataclysmic levels, we need Nouwen's witness as a man who held raw anguish alongside tangible hope. A man who was tempted and tried, yet who clung to the power of the cross despite it all. In a time when corrosive social media and the allure of digital distraction conspire to keep us from being people of any depth whatsoever, Nouwen's deep inner well reminds us there are cleaner waters to drink from.

Our world is increasingly divided over issues of sexuality and faith, but Nouwen's legacy provides a way forward. His life testifies to a spirituality of inclusion that does not ignore the authority of Scripture or the challenges of discipleship but embraces them as part of a dynamic, loving journey. As someone who embraced both his faith and his vulnerabilities, Nouwen invites us to build communities that truly embody the heart of the gospel: love, humility, and radical hospitality. His example reminds us that every person, regardless of their sexual orientation, is called to—and capable of—a deep, transformative relationship with God and profound contribution to the church.

Nouwen's life should also prompt us to nurture the gifts and calling of our LGBTQ+ neighbors. To cultivate spaces not just where they can attend and tithe but are invited to step into their God-given identities. This is more than welcoming people to warm pews and chairs on Sunday morning. If we have people in our circle who experience gender dysphoria or same-sex attraction and who have set those things apart in trust and faithfulness to God, our circle should be a place where their gifts will be nurtured, championed, and released, not snuffed out.

REVIVALIST FIRE

Nouwen isn't the only figure in recent church history who challenges me to make my table a little bigger. If the church is experiencing a crisis of depth, it is also experiencing a crisis of mission. Culture wars, political idolatry, and distraction of all kinds have attempted to pour water on the fire of God's work in the world. But this man stoked the fires of revival in his time.

In 1967 while traveling the California desert and tripping on LSD, a gay hippie found Jesus, and America would never be the same. He embraced Christianity in a way that would reshape the landscape of modern evangelicalism. His conversion and passionate preaching captured the hearts of many, drawing in people who felt alienated from the traditional church and finding resonance with those looking for authentic encounters with God.

His charismatic preaching and captivating personality drew thousands to Christ, particularly among the countercultural youth of his day. His impact on the modern church was so profound that we feel its echoes to this day. In fact, this hippie preacher would go on to help pioneer not one but two of the most influential church movements in American evangelicalism. He inspired and collaborated with Chuck Smith, helping forge what would become Calvary Chapel's network of churches, and later he partnered with John Wimber to help launch the Vineyard Church movement.

His name was Lonnie Frisbee.

Frisbee was a pivotal figure in the Jesus movement of the 1960s and 1970s. He had a recent surge of recognition thanks to the popular 2022 Christian movie *Jesus Revolution*. While I appreciate those filmmakers for not writing Lonnie out of the story completely, as historians have often done, I was discouraged by the pieces of Lonnie's life they chose to omit.

Throughout his life Lonnie struggled with his sexuality. Though he identified as gay, he believed that his sexuality needed to be surrendered to Christ's vision of sexuality as revealed in the Scriptures. He experienced profound inner conflict, wrestling with his sexual orientation amid a religious climate that largely rejected its LGBTQ+ neighbors. In his lifetime, as in ours, the broader evangelical movement was often unsympathetic, treating LGBTQ+ individuals as outsiders at best and monsters at worst. As a result, Lonnie lived much of his life in secrecy, attempting to reconcile his faith and ministry with temptations he was forced to wrestle with in private.

This private wrestling eventually led to private sin. Frisbee ended up marrying a woman with whom he was honest about his temptations. He also reportedly sought help and accountability from pastoral contemporaries, but none were equipped to support him. He eventually stopped being faithful to his wife and had multiple affairs with men. There is no excuse for this. But it's worth remembering that when we are forced to wrestle in private, when vulnerability is discouraged and empathy is lean, we are all more capable of self-destructive behavior than we want to believe.

Lonnie Frisbee was eventually asked to step away from the ministries he was involved in. Eventually he contracted HIV, a disease that led to his death. After his sexual indiscretions were revealed, both Chuck Smith and John Wimber significantly decreased their public mentions of Frisbee and stopped associating with him. Slowly he was written out of the story of the Jesus movement.

There have been some attempts by modern progressive Christians to claim Frisbee as a queer Christian icon who embraced a progressive perspective on sex and gay marriage. However, all reports indicate the opposite. Frisbee never viewed his sexual struggle as something that pleased God. He did not have a clear conscience about infidelity or his sex with men. And at the end of his life, he returned to devotion to the Scriptures and Christ. Frisbee's last days were spent praying for another outpouring of the Holy Spirit to stoke the fires of revival. He died in March 1993.[3]

I first heard about Lonnie Frisbee, almost by divine providence, when I was in Bible college and entering ministry. I was attending Calvary Chapel University. During this time, I had a friend with a flair for the radical, and he told me if I was going to attend Calvary Chapel's Bible college, I should know about the man who started it all.

As a closeted man, I was moved to my core by the story of this gay hippie preacher who shaped the modern church. I was both inspired by his impact and fearful of his downfall, fearful the same would happen to me. What moved me and challenged me the most was how profoundly God moved through Frisbee's ministry. Somehow, someway, Frisbee's being gay didn't stop a dramatic move of God in his time. Even with his moral failings and unpopular temptations, God worked through this man to reach a people group few Christians of the day had any interest in reaching.

LOOKING TO THE FUTURE

Lonnie Frisbee and Henri Nouwen are radiant examples of people who, despite profound inner struggles with their sexuality, made an undeniable impact on the church. Frisbee, a key figure in the Jesus movement and charismatic renewal, played a major role in bringing thousands to faith through his passionate evangelism, particularly among the counterculture youth of the 1960s and 1970s. Henri Nouwen became one of the most beloved spiritual writers of the twentieth century, deeply influencing Christians with his vulnerability, theological depth, and insights on loneliness, love, and grace.

Both started their most influential work in the 1960s. Both died in the mid-1990s. They served as prophetic images for the vocation of the church: radical mission on one hand, deep formation on the other. Both men held theologically historic perspectives on sexuality and wrestled with their identities in an era when the church forced them into hiding.

They suffered in dark closets. They often suffered alone. They continued to bear witness to the luminous beauty of Christ despite their suffering.

If the church were to embrace rather than sideline queer people today, it could create a space where individuals like Frisbee and Nouwen wouldn't need to choose between their callings and honesty about their struggles. By fostering a spirit of orthodox inclusivity, the church could free many from shame and the fear of rejection, allowing them to serve fully and authentically. We might see a flourishing of diverse voices and gifts that would enrich the church, much as Nouwen and Frisbee did.

Imagine the impact if we had more Nouwens and Frisbees today, people who are free to bring their whole selves to the church. A church that received its LGBTQ+ neighbors could not only heal deep wounds but also open itself up to be transformed by the faith, resilience, and devotion of those who have often been on its margins. All of this is possible without redefining what the church has unilaterally taught to be true for the last two thousand years regarding sex, marriage, and gender.

WE DON'T WANT TO "SHOUT ALL THE MORE"

In the story of Jesus and the blind beggar, the blind beggar "shouted all the more" over the disciples' rebuke of him (Luke 18:39). I applaud his courage. But after this encounter, it would not be appropriate for more blind beggars down the road to have to "shout all the more" to be brought into intimacy with Jesus. After Jesus moved beyond the dehumanizing barriers placed between the blind man and himself, I can't imagine he would be pleased to see his followers re-erecting those barriers.

What God reveals to us he holds us to. He does not want his children to have to shout above the clamor and noise of un-Christlike rebukes from his followers. And, truthfully, we are tired from shouting. We are tired of having to justify our existence. We are tired of being loved as long as we hide. Jesus does not model this in his ministry, and we should not model this in our churches.

As I write this book, I think about all the LGBTQ+ Jesus-followers who have graced my life over the years. Some hold to a historic perspective on sex, marriage, and gender; some hold to a progressive view; some are still figuring it out. But what they all have in common is their resilient quest to know Jesus and love him.

They have had to work a little harder to reconcile their identities with Jesus. They have had to study a little deeper to make sense of theology and experience. They have had to keep their mouths shut when ignorant things were said about them or people who experience what they experience. They have had to question if they belong in church, belong with Jesus, if the work of the cross extends to them.

I think of my best friend, whose relationship with Jesus inspires him to show up on the front lines for the most at-risk youth in his city, day in and day out. I think of the trans high schoolers I know who go to church even when their parents don't, who arrive early to help set up and stay late to help tear down. I think of one friend who has turned the wounds of transitioning and detransitioning into a tremendous resource for curious Christians.

I think of one friend who has committed his life to celibacy and the work of equipping the church theologically and with love.

I think of someone I pastored who came to church the Sunday after our local Pride rally and wept with me as they shared stories of being screamed at by Christians picketing the event. Then they sang on our worship team that morning with joy. They wept because of how Jesus was misrepresented. They sang with joy because they know who Jesus actually is.

Each of these individuals has fought, wrestled, doubted, failed, and pressed on more than just about any other follower of Jesus I know. They inspire me to take up my cross, to think deeper, to love harder, and to recklessly follow Jesus. They are my heroes. And they should not have to shout above ungodly barriers to belong in the church.

If you have made it this far, dear reader, I thank you. Thank you for caring, for loving, for working, and for learning. We have come so far, but we still have so far to go. It is not too late for the LGBTQ+ people in our churches to be loved and received by us as we all are by Christ. And it's not too late for our LGBTQ+ neighbors outside our churches to find and follow Jesus.

So go. Be sent out as Jesus was sent out. Bear witness to the beauty, goodness, truth, and love of Jesus. Courageously hold fast to the truth of Scripture and the beauty of orthodoxy. May love be the loudest noise we make. May our tables get bigger. Jesus is making his appeal through us.

Let's get to work.

REFLECTION QUESTIONS

1. What steps can you take to make your table bigger in your home, your family, or your church?
2. Who are the LGBTQ+ people today you know personally who have impacted your life?
3. How can we invite our queer loved ones to the table without revising traditional teachings of Scripture?

ACKNOWLEDGMENTS

To my sweet wife, Kelsey, you are the surest sign of God's grace to me, and my favorite part about being alive. To my family: Dad, Brennan, Paul, Lainey, Ryan, Callum, Miranda, Ruby, and Kristi, I love you more than words can say. To my exceedingly wise and patient editor, Rachel, and the rest of the team at InterVarsity Press, thank you for giving this book a shot. To Jordan, Eli, Lynette, AJ, Quinn, Lane, Kate, Preston, Josh, Russ, Isaac, Christian, Alex, Eli Jr., Autumn, Vi, Aaron, the crews at Open Table Church and Red Hills Church, my Western Seminary cohort, and those I'm sure I'll be kicking myself for forgetting: You have loved this neighbor into Gospel wholeness. This book is indebted to you.

NOTES

INTRODUCTION

[1]Matt Lavietes, "Nearly 30% of Gen Z Adults Identify as LGBTQ, National Survey Finds," NBC News, January 24, 2024, www.nbcnews.com/nbc-out/out-news/nearly-30-gen-z-adults-identify-lgbtq-national-survey-finds-rcna135510.

1. THE FELT TENSION

[1]A. J. Swoboda, *The Gift of Thorns: Jesus, the Flesh, and the War for Our Wants* (Zondervan, 2024), 25-26.

[2]Andrew Marin, *Us Versus Us: The Untold Story of Religion and the LGBT Community* (NavPress, 2016), 36.

[3]Marin, *Us Versus Us*, 54.

[4]Marin, *Us Versus Us*, 31, 45.

[5]Preston Sprinkle, *Does the Bible Support Same Sex Marriage? 21 Conversations from a Historically Christian View* (David C Cook, 2023), 181.

[6]Greg Lukianoff and Jonathan Haidt, *The Coddling of the American Mind: How Good Intentions and Bad Ideas Are Setting Up a Generation for Failure* (Penguin, 2018), 23-25.

[7]I'd recommend Preston Sprinkle, *People to Be Loved: Why Homosexuality Is Not Just an Issue* (Zondervan, 2015), and *Embodied: Transgender Identities, the Church, and What the Bible Has to Say* (David C Cook, 2021); Christopher West, *Theology of the Body for Beginners: Rediscovering the Meaning of Life, Love, Sex, and Gender*, rev. ed. (Ascension, 2009); and Wesley Hill, *Washed and Waiting: Reflections on Christian Faithfulness and Homosexuality* (Zondervan, 2016). These are great primers for understanding the traditional ethic.

[8]N. T. Wright, *Not Just Good, But Beautiful* (Plough Publishing, 2015), 88.

[9]West, *Theology of the Body*, 19.

[10]This admittedly raises questions about intersexed people, who are born with both male and female chromosomes and genitalia. While we can't explore that issue in depth here, I'd recommend this article as a helpful resource: Preston Sprinkle, "Sex, Gender, and Transgender Experiences: Part 6—What about Intersex?" Center

for Faith, Sexuality and Gender, August 26, 2019, www.centerforfaith.com/blog-sex-gender-and-transgender-experiences-part-6-what-about-intersex.

2. HIDING TO BE LOVED

[1]I wrote about this experience in my first book, Tony Scarcello, *Regenerate: Following Jesus After Deconstruction* (Wipf and Stock, 2020).

[2]Spencer Macnaughton, "Religious Trauma Still Haunts Millions of LGBTQ+ Americans," NBC News, January 28, 2024, www.nbcnews.com/nbc-out/out-health-and-wellness/millions-lgbtq-americans-religious-trauma-psychiatrists-want-help-rcna135728.

[3]"Statistics on LGBTQ+ Youth and OYA," Office of Inclusion and Intercultural Relations," Oregon.gov, www.oregon.gov/oya/oiir/pages/lgbtq.aspx. Accessed August 16, 2025.

[4]Bridget Eileen Rivera, *Heavy Burdens: Seven Ways LGBTQ+ Christians Experience Harm in the Church* (Brazos, 2021), 50.

[5]M. Robert Mulholland Jr., *The Deeper Journey: The Spirituality of Discovering Your True Self* (InterVarsity Press, 2006), 119-120.

3. THE HISTORY OF HARM

[1]I have written about this experience for The Center for Faith, Sexuality, and Gender. Tony Scarcello, "Is the Church Getting Safer for LGBTQ People?," January 12, 2022, https://centerforfaith.com/blog-is-the-church-getting-safer-for-lgbtq-people/.

[2]David Bennett, *A War of Loves* (Zondervan, 2018).

[3]Ron Alexander, "In Key West, the Latest 'Invaders' Have Set Off a Backlash," *The New York Times*, April 7, 1979, www.nytimes.com/1979/04/07/archives/in-key-west-the-latest-invaders-have-set-off-a-backlash-many-are.html.

[4]Minyvonne Burke, "Texas Pastor Says Gay People Should Be 'Shot in the Back of the Head' in Shocking Sermon," NBC News, June 9, 2022, www.nbcnews.com/nbc-out/out-news/texas-pastor-says-gay-people-shot-back-head-shocking-sermon-rcna32748.

[5]Steve Helling, "The Colorado Springs Shooting Is Latest in Long Line of Attacks at LGBTQ+ Establishments," *People*, November 22, 2022, https://people.com/crime/colorado-springs-shooting-latest-attack-lgbtq-establishments.

[6]Rich Barlow, "How the AIDS Crisis Became a Moral Debate," *BU Today*, December 3, 2015, www.bu.edu/articles/2015/anthony-petro-after-the-wrath-of-god.

[7]"Religion and Religious Groups," in *The Social Impact Of AIDS In The United States*, ed. A. R. Jonsen and J. Stryker (National Academies Press, 1993), www.ncbi.nlm.nih.gov/books/NBK234566.

[8]"Jerry Falwell on the 'Homosexual Revolution' (1981)," The American Yawp Reader, August 13, 1981, www.americanyawp.com/reader/29-the-triumph-of-the-right/jerry-falwell-on-the-homosexual-revolution-1981.

[9]Greg Johnson, *Still Time to Care: What We Can Learn from the Church's Failed Attempt to Cure Homosexuality* (Zondervan, 2021), 13.

[10]Tony Scarcello, "Prioritizing Mercy When Discussing Sexuality," The Center for Faith, Sexuality & Gender, April 5, 2024, https://www.centerforfaith.com/blog-prioritizing-mercy-when-discussing-sexuality.

[11]A. J. Swoboda and Nijay K. Gupta, *Slow Theology: Eight Practices for Resilient Faith in a Turbulent World* (Brazos Press, 2025).

4. CASUALTIES OF CULTURE WAR

[1]It is important to note that their comments are far from reflecting how most evangelicals felt about 9/11. See their discussion here: "Jerry Falwell and Pat Robertson Blame 9/11 on Organizations Like People For the American Way," peoplefor.org, YouTube, www.youtube.com/watch?v=kMkBgA9_oQ4&t=4s.

[2]Associated Press, "Swaggart Apologizes for Talk of Killing Gays," NBC News, September 22, 2004, www.nbcnews.com/id/wbna6074380.

[3]*Shiny Happy People: A Teenage Holy War*, directed by Cori Shepherd and Nicole Newnham, Amazon Studios, 2025, www.amazon.com/Shiny-Happy-People-Teenage-Holy/dp/B0FD3G7PP7.

[4]Dallas Willard, *Spirit of the Disciplines: Understanding How God Changes Lives* (Harper One, 1988), 13.

[5]Giles Crouch, "The Pace of World Change Is Accelerating," *Silver,* March 24, 2021, https://silvermagazine.ca/the-pace-of-world-change-is-accelerating.

[6]Edwin Friedman, *Failure of Nerve: Leadership in the Age of the Quick Fix* (Seabury, 1999), 57.

[7]Unless, of course, we are talking about fear of the Lord.

[8]In his book *The Party Crasher: How Jesus Disrupts Politics as Usual and Redeems Our Partisan Divide* (Multnomah, 2024), Joshua Ryan Butler convincingly argues that there are actually four main political movements at work in the states. Still, they tend to be divided down the line, two against two.

[9]Jonathan Haidt, *The Happiness Hypothesis: Finding Modern Truth in Ancient Wisdom* (Basic, 2006), 242.

[10]Philip Rieff, *The Triumph of the Therapeutic: Uses of Faith after Freud* (Harper & Row, 1966).

[11]Richard Beck, *Hunting Magic Eels: Recovering an Enchanted Faith in a Skeptical Age* (Broadleaf, 2021), 23.

[12]See Charles Taylor's seminal work, *A Secular Age* (Belknap, 2018), 452.

[13]James K. A. Smith, *Awaiting the Kingdom: Reforming Public Theology* (Baker Academic, 2017), 29.

[14]Jim Davis et al., *The Great Dechurching: Who's Leaving, Why Are They Going, and What Will It Take to Bring Them Back* (Zondervan, 2023), 5.

[15]Though recent data is suggesting a hopeful shift in these trends.

[16]"How U.S. Religious Composition Has Changed in Recent Decades," in Modeling the Future of Religion in America (report), Pew Research Center, September 13, 2022, www.pewresearch.org/religion/2022/09/13/how-u-s-religious-composition-has-changed-in-recent-decades.

5. MORAL PANIC

[1]Saint Augustine of Hippo, *City of God*, 15.22.

[2]Preston Sprinkle, *Exiles: Church in the Shadow of Empire* (David C Cook, 2024), 11.

[3]Esa McCaulley, *Reading While Black: African American Biblical Interpretation as an Exercise in Hope* (IVP Academic, 2020), 149.

[4]Joshua Ryan Butler, *The Party Crasher: How Jesus Disrupts Politics as Usual and Redeems Our Partisan Divide* (Multnomah, 2024), 25.

[5]A. J. Swoboda, *The Gift of Thorns: Jesus, the Flesh, and the War for Our Wants* (Zondervan, 2024), 72.

[6]See Dietrich Bonhoeffer, *Ethics* (Touchstone, 1949), chap. 1.

[7]Edwin Friedman, *A Failure of Nerve: Leadership in the Age of the Quick Fix* (Seabury, 199), 53.

[8]Ben Sasse, *Them: Why We Hate Each Other—and How to Heal* (St. Martin's, 2018), 4.

[9]Friedman, *Failure of Nerve*, 53.

[10]Tim Jonze, "'I'm Just Trying to Make the World a Little Brighter': How the Culture Wars Hijacked Drag Queen Story Hour," *The Guardian*, August 11, 2022, www.theguardian.com/culture/2022/aug/11/im-just-trying-to-make-the-world-a-little-brighter-how-the-culture-wars-hijacked-drag-queen-story-hour.

[11]Friedman, *Failure of Nerve*, 54

[12]Friedman, *Failure of Nerve*, 53.

[13]Friedman, *Failure of Nerve*, 54.

[14]Friedman, *Failure of Nerve*, 54.

[15]CNN, "Flashback: McCain Tells Supporter Obama As 'a Decent . . . '," YouTube, February 19, 2015, www.youtube.com/watch?v=JijenjANqAk.

[16]I highly recommend Steve Cuss, *Managing Leadership Anxiety: Yours and Theirs* (Thomas Nelson, 2019), for a Christian perspective on the cycle of anxiety and undifferentiated leadership.

[17]In many Christian spaces, LGBTQ+ believers divide themselves into different camps. To be with Side A is to say that God blesses, permits, and approves of same-sex sexual relationships and gender transitions. Side A attempts to be a Christian champion

for same-sex marriages and transgender identities. Side B asserts there is no moral compromise in referring to oneself as gay or queer, or to experience gender dysphoria, but still holds to the traditional, historic Christian sexual ethic. While they would say same-sex attraction and gender dysphoria are not in and of themselves sinful, they are nonetheless byproducts of a world marred by sin. So they would advocate for celibacy or mixed-orientation marriages.

6. UNGODLY THEOLOGY

[1]A. W. Tozer, *Knowledge of the Holy* (Harper Collins, 1978), 1.

[2]Karl Barth, *The Epistle to the Romans*, 6th ed. (Oxford University Press, 1968), 51.

[3]Mark A. Yarhouse, *Understanding Sexual Identity: A Resource for Youth Ministry* (Zondervan, 2013), 47.

[4]Emily Hunter McGowin, *Households of Faith: Practicing Family in the Kingdom of God* (InterVarsity Press, 2025).

[5]Preston Sprinkle, *People to Be Loved: Why Homosexuality Is Not Just an Issue* (Zondervan, 2015); Preston Sprinkle, *Embodied: Transgender Identities, the Church, and What the Bible Has to Say* (David C. Cook, 2019).

[6]Gregory Coles, *Single, Gay, Christian: A Personal Journey of Faith and Sexual Identity* (InterVarsity Press, 2017); David Bennett, *War of Loves: The Unexpected Story of a Gay Activist Discovering Jesus* (Zondervan, 2018).

[7]Greg Johnson, *Still Time to Care: What We Can Learn from the Church's Failed Attempt to Cure Homosexuality* (Zondervan, 2021).

[8]There is a fascinating documentary on Netflix about this called *Pray Away*, directed by Kristine Stolakis, 2021.

[9]The scope of Johnson's book is mostly focused on same-sex attraction. The ethics and practice of reparative therapy for same-sex attraction is an entirely different bag than for gender dysphoria. There are many people who experience gender dysphoria that have found reprieve through the right therapy. However, one must always use tremendous discretion when taking this to therapy.

[10]Johnson, *Still Time to Care*, 53.

[11]C. S. Lewis, *Surprised by Joy* (HarperOne, 1955), 97.

[12]Alister McGrath, *C. S. Lewis: A Life* (Tyndale Elevate, 2013), 61-62.

[13]C. S. Lewis, *The Collected Letters of C. S. Lewis*, vol. 3, *Narnia, Cambridge, and Joy, 1950–1963* (HarperOne, 2009), 471.

[14]Richard B. Hays, *The Moral Vision of the New Testament: Community, Cross, New Creation* (HarperOne, 1996), 46.

7. REPENT AND BELIEVE

[1]Jennifer Lee, "Max Lucado Apologises for 'Disrespectful' 2004 Sermon Denouncing Homosexuality," Christian Today, February 16, 2021, www.christiantoday.com/news/max-lucado-apologises-for-disrespectful-2004-sermon-denouncing-homosexuality.

[2]Steve Warren, "Max Lucado Issues Apology After Coming Under Fire by LGBT Community," CBN, February 11, 2021, https://cbn.com/news/us/max-lucado-issues-apology-after-coming-under-fire-lgbt-community.

[3]Check out Patrick Schreiner, *The Kingdom of God and the Glory of the Cross* (Crossway, 2018); N. T. Wright, *How God Became King* (HarperOne, 2016); or Dallas Willard, *The Divine Conspiracy* (Harper, 1998).

[4]Amy-Jill Levine, *Short Stories by Jesus: The Enigmatic Parables of a Controversial Rabbi* (HarperOne, 2014), 25.

[5]Matthew Bates, *Salvation by Allegiance Alone: Rethinking Faith, Works, and the Gospel of Jesus the King* (Baker Academic, 2017), chap. 1.

[6]Charles H. Spurgeon, *Spurgeon at His Best: Over 2,200 Striking Quotations from the World's Most Exhaustive and Widely-Read Sermon Series* (Baker, 1988).

[7]I have also written further on this: Tony Scarcello, "Prioritizing Mercy When Discussing Sexuality," The Center for Faith, Sexuality & Gender, April 5, 2024, https://centerforfaith.com/blog-prioritizing-mercy-when-discussing-sexuality/.

[8]Shout-out to Eugene Peterson, author of *A Long Obedience in the Same Direction: Discipleship in an Instant Society* (InterVarsity Press, 1980).

[9]Charles Taylor, *The Ethics of Authenticity* (Harvard University Press, 1992), 29.

[10]Christopher Watkin, *Biblical Critical Theory: How the Bible's Unfolding Story Makes Sense of Modern Life and Culture* (Zondervan Academic, 2022), 43.

[11]Carl Trueman, *Strange New World : How Thinkers and Activists Redefined Identity and Sparked the Sexual Revolution* (Crossway, 2022), 22.

8. THE FRUITS OF REPENTANCE

[1]Randy Alcorn, *The Grace and Truth Paradox: Responding with Christlike Balance* (Multnomah, 2003), 17.

[2]John R. W. Stott, *Christian Counter-Culture: The Message of the Sermon on the Mount* (InterVarsity Press, 1978), 51.

[3]Jim Manney, *The Prayer of Examen: Ignatian Wisdom for Our Lives Today* (Loyola Press, 2010), 7.

9. CAN I GET A WITNESS?

[1]Lyndon B. Johnson and Billy Graham recorded phone call, October 20, 1964, Miller Center Archive, University of Virginia, citation 5926.

[2]David Benner, *Surrender to Love: Discovering the Heart of Christian Spirituality* (InterVarsity Press, 2015), 38.

[3]Gerald L. Sittser, *Water from a Deep Well: Christian Spirituality from Early Martyrs to Modern Missionaries* (InterVarsity Press, 2007), 51-52.

[4]Eugene H. Peterson, *The Pastor: A Memoir* (HarperOne, 2011), 40.

[5]Sittser, *Water from a Deep Well*, 61-62.

[6]Certainly, nonsecular people experience anxiety and depression as well, yet several compelling studies have shown that nonreligious people are more prone to these experiences. See Shankar Vedantam, "Hidden Brain: Does Going to Church Improve Your Mental Health?" NPR, November 5, 2019, www.npr.org/2019/11/05/776270553/hidden-brain-does-going-to-church-improve-your-mental-health.

[7]"2023 U.S. National Survey on the Mental Health of LGBTQ+ Young People," The Trevor Project, 2023, www.thetrevorproject.org/survey-2023.

[8]Sittser, *Water from a Deep Well*, 63.

[9]Dionysius, *Eusebius, Ecclesiastical History*, 7.22.

[10]For further study on this, see Tom Holland's *Dominion: How the Christian Revolution Remade the World* (Basic, 2019); David Bentley Hart's *Atheist Delusions: The Christian Revolution and Its Fashionable Enemies* (Yale University Press, 2010); and Glen Scrivener's *The Air We Breathe: How We All Came to Believe in Freedom, Kindness, Progress, and Equality* (Good Book Company, 2022).

[11]Andrew Marin, *Us Versus Us: The Untold Story of Religion and the LGBT Community* (NavPress, 2016).

10. WHEN SOMEONE YOU LOVE COMES OUT

[1]Curt Thompson, *The Soul of Shame: Retelling the Stories We Believe About Ourselves* (InterVarsity Press, 2015), 138.

[2]Shankar Vedantam, "Hidden Brain: Does Going to Church Improve Your Mental Health?" NPR, November 5, 2019, www.npr.org/2019/11/05/776270553/hidden-brain-does-going-to-church-improve-your-mental-health; W. J. Strawbridge et al., "Religious Attendance Increases Survival by Improving and Maintaining Good Health Behaviors, Mental Health, and Social Relationships," *Annals of Behavioral Medicine* 23, no. 1 (Winter 2001): 68-74. http:doi.org/10.1207/s15324796abm2301_10.

[3]Christopher West, "Art & the New Evangelization: How Beauty Will Save the World," The Imaginative Conservative, September 22, 2024, https://theimaginativeconservative.org/2024/09/art-new-evangelization-beauty-christopher-west.html.

[4]Fred B. Craddock, *Luke*, Interpretation: A Bible Commentary for Teaching and Preaching (Westminster John Knox, 1990), 104.

[5]Eugene Peterson, *Eat This Book: A Conversation in the Art of Spiritual Reading* (Eerdmans, 2009), 18.

11. A BIGGER TABLE

[1]For further reading, check out Michael W. Higgins and Kevin Burns, *Genius Born of Anguish: The Life and Legacy of Henri Nouwen* (Paulist, 2012).

[2]Henri J. M. Nouwen, *The Wounded Healer: Ministry in Contemporary Society* (Image/Doubleday, 1972), 70.

[3]For all of this and more, check out the excellent documentary *Frisbee: The Life and Death of a Hippie Preacher*, written and directed by David Di Sabatino, 2005.